Speak II Me:
A Black Father's Journey Raising a Son on the Autism Spectrum

by Jamiyl Samuels

with contributions from Tracy-Ann Samuels, MSW

©2022 by **Jamiyl Samuels** for **A Humble Work Publishing**

All rights reserved.

Cover design by **Jacqueline Stallworth** for **10.30 Designs**

This book is based on actual events. (*) denotes the names that have been changed to protect the guilty.

No part of this book may be reproduced or transmitted in any form or by any means, electronic or mechanical, including photocopying, recording, or by any information storage or retrieval system, without permission in writing from the author.

ISBN: 978-1-7378108-2-7
ISBN 13: 978-0-5782853-5-1

DEDICATION

For Trey:

Your life has inspired me in ways I did not think possible. I thank God for creating you just as you are. I thank Him for granting me the clarity to see the greatness He made in you. You are brilliant, you are more than a diagnosis. You are unstoppable. You are extraordinary. You are my legacy.

ACKNOWLEDGMENTS

I must acknowledge my wife Tracy-Ann. Your consistent words of encouragement and motivation fuel me. Thank you for your strength. Your tireless advocacy for our son renewed my faith. Your unflinching love, perseverance, insight, and dedication to him in the face of unbelievable uncertainty blows my mind. I am truly honored, and humbled to have you by my side during this journey. A mother's love is unwavering. I am grateful to be a witness. My love for you knows no bounds.

Aja: Thank you for speaking to Trey. Thank you for loving him. Thank you for being who you are. Thank you for inspiring me. There is no responsibility I take more pride in than being your Dad. I love you.

Ms. Knight: for setting the wheels in motion.

The Neuro diverse community: It is my honor to fight for your acceptance in an often-cruel world. Let us normalize empathy and understanding over misinformation and judgement.

CONTENTS

SPEAK II ME

If you truly love someone,
you help that person

PROLOGUE

I am my son's hero.

He wants to do everything I do.

More times than I can count he directs my attention to his newly grown mustache and rubs his hand along his chin, showing off a beard that exists only in his imagination.

"I'm gonna shave too," he said, flashing a smile that exuded as much confidence as naiveté.

I am my son's hero.

He wants to drive just like me. He is 15 years old now, but periodically lets me know that he is one year away from being able to officially learn. He sits in the front seat now when we drive together. I know he is watching my every move anticipating his time.

I am my son's hero.

I was in a bowling league; he likes to bowl. I played little league baseball; he played baseball in the local league. He loves golf and soccer as well. Go figure.

I am my son's hero.

Only a child that looks up to his father would come around him at random times just to say:

"Hey, Daddy."

"Yes, son."

"I love you, Daddy."

"I love you too, son."

Only a boy who reveres his father would randomly rub the upper back of his old man smiling from ear to ear.

I am my son's hero.

I know how much he looks up to me. I know how much he enjoys being around me and vice versa. He is my progeny, my heir, the future of my last name.

I am my son's hero.

Giving Trey my name was not an option. His was an original choice of the four names I wrote down as a teenager. Jamiyl Jr. was also one of those names but, like my mother, my wife wanted our son to have his own identity.

I am my son's hero.

I will never not want the job. Being charged with the

responsibility of building and cultivating a legacy, to lead the next generation of a young Black man by the example I set, knowing he is watching how I conduct myself daily, is a duty I proudly embrace.

One day my son grew silent. A once happily babbling baby became a child of few words. Instead of being suspicious about the sudden change, I believed he was just a quiet child. I didn't really socialize with other kids in school until around the third grade. I thought all I had to do was put him in a classroom around other children and he would start talking.

My wife Tracy-Ann, his mom, is a social worker. She works with developmentally delayed and medically fragile youth on a regular basis. She saw signs in Trey that looked like the clients she worked with on her job.

Denial is a funny thing sometimes. It is the foundation for the building of resentment, the seed for the growth of clouded judgement, creates perfectly formed excuses for inaction, formulates an answer for the unexplainable, and suspends your belief in what is real.

For years Trey walked around unable to communicate effectively. He was five years old when he was diagnosed with Mixed Expressive Receptive Language Disorder and seven years old when he was officially diagnosed with autism spectrum disorder (ASD). I had no choice but to step up and be the man my son was depending on. To prove me worthy of the pedestal he put me on. To stop thinking about myself and put his needs first.

My son is my hero.

Another random thing he does is stand with his shoulder next to mine, a constant reminder that he is almost as tall as I am. Yet I feel like I am the one who is trying to measure up to him.

BLESSING

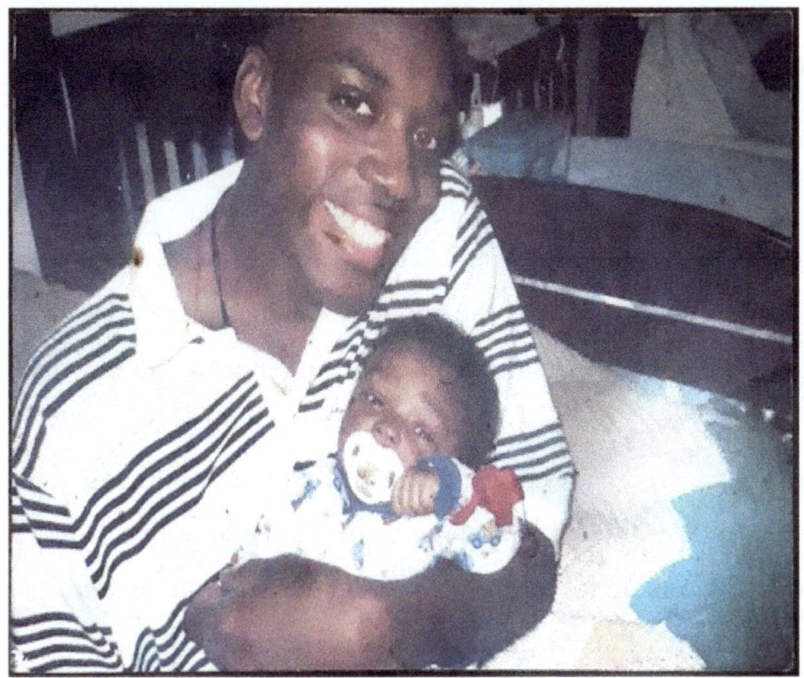

MARCH 10, 2007.

I heard the cry of my first born for the first time. Trey Amani spoke to me through this sound. He spoke to my inner being, that child that was ready to be the man my father was not for me. He would be my opportunity to break a generational curse. I waited 28 years to speak to my child. Unfortunately, an exhilarating high was preceded by a devastating low.

When my wife Tracy-Ann got pregnant for the first time we were seven months into our marriage. While it was important for us to be wed before starting a family, our intention was to enjoy at least two years together without children.

God had other plans, however, as a positive pregnancy test was my wife's Valentine's Day gift to me.

The next few weeks were a blur. We could not contain our excitement. We told family members, close friends, and co-workers.

Nine weeks into the pregnancy, Tracy-Ann began experiencing severe abdominal pains. For the next week she complained about unusual cramping in her stomach and sharp pains near her groin area. These complaints were brushed off, cavalierly dismissed by the doctor charged with her care. It was "all in her mind," he said. Based on the weekly ultrasound the heart was beating fine. She was accused of "thinking too much" by a man whom we trusted to think for us. To fill in the blanks of gray areas we had yet to navigate.

When my wife called me from her job complaining of the same pain, I took her to the emergency room. After being discharged by the ER physician, her doctor finally prescribed two weeks of bed rest. When he cleared her to return to work, it was only a few days before the pain returned and we were back in the emergency room. When we called our doctor to notify him, he tried to blame her for returning to work, failing to remember it was on his order that she had done so.

APRIL 12, 2006.

We arrived for our scheduled appointment with the doctor a bit shaken from the crisis Tracy-Ann experienced just one day ago. We were anxious to see the heartbeat we witnessed many times before, our confirmation that everything was going to be alright.

This time, however, we did not see any movement. The doctor moved the ultrasound device around slightly, but for some reason we could not spot any activity in the grainy black-and-white image on the screen. He continued to circle the wand around, still there was nothing. It never took this long before to locate the fetus. I searched his eyes and saw panic, fear. And as the realization set in that there was no more life in the womb of my wife's body, he simply removed the device, turned around, and walked out of the room.

We stared at the screen for a few more minutes. The silence between us was deafening, then excruciating as our worst fears started to hit us. We were not physicians, but we eventually began to grasp what the doctor failed to tell us before he disappeared.

I remember reaching for paper towels and helping my wife clean up. I was in disbelief. As I helped her off the table the tears began to fall.

How could this happen? Why did this happen? Valid questions in the aftermath of this shocking occurrence. There was no one in the room to respond. I walked towards the doorway in search of answers. I peered down the hallway to my right and saw that our doctor's office door was closed. The guy that told us we were 'thinking too much' and to 'stop worrying', was nowhere to be found when we needed reassurance. That is because he could not provide any. He gave us bad advice. He was negligent.

I was in a fog of my own. The memory of what happened next is hazy. I do remember when the doctor finally opened the door to his office one of my questions was about Tracy-Ann's bloodwork and if it was checked. His affirmative response was rushed as if he was caught off guard by my query. He made no eye contact.

I truly believe he never checked her bloodwork. It angered me to no end that he did not apologize or offer any words of sympathy. Not that we would have accepted, but there was no effort made to console us or offer any information on what to do next.

In the days that followed I watched my wife cry for long hours. It was a helpless feeling. We agonized over what caused her miscarriage. Breaking the news to our family members was extremely painful. I became most upset, however, when I was alone with my thoughts. Wondering what we could have done differently. It's an unusual kind of torture, the hindsight. So much clarity in looking back after the consequences of mistakes have materialized.

I can only speak to what Tracy-Ann shared with me: the insufferable guilt about not following her instincts, allowing the doctor to dismiss her questions and concerns about the pains she was feeling. The indescribable feeling of failure to protect her fetus. The thought that she could have lost her life if she did not seek proper medical attention.

Adding insult to injury is being days away from surpassing the first trimester, an important benchmark in the journey of childbirth. It is a grief I have buried… until times like these when I think about it. Writing about it. What could have been. If I felt like this, I could not imagine the anguish or the psychological trauma my wife was dealing with.

Tracy-Ann always wanted twins. It was talked about so often that it became a running joke. Really, what were the chances? From wishful thinking to learning there was a possibility that she lost two fetuses, not knowing about the other one… it was difficult to fathom. They say sometimes one fetus hides behind the other in the womb out of sight of the ultrasound.

If this was true, God knew best. They were with Him.

It is what I tell myself time and again when my mind wanders to those moments. Maybe we don't try again if we have twins. The way I watched my wife mourn I did not think we would revisit getting pregnant anytime soon. There was no limit to the length of time I was willing to wait to allow her to heal. That period did not last very long.

One thing I will say, Tracy-Ann did not sit idly by and wallow in self-pity. We saw a specialist at New York Presbyterian seeking the answers we did not get from the doctor that abandoned us. A battery of diagnostic blood tests revealed that her body was fighting against the 'foreign objects' growing inside her womb. The specialist also informed us that her blood was clotting, cutting off oxygen to her uterus.

It was confirmation of what I knew in my heart: the doctor never checked her bloodwork. If he only paid attention my wife would have been prescribed the blood thinning medication she needed. It was equal parts maddening and eye-opening. At least we knew what happened was no fault of our own.

JUNE 2006.

After all we went through, we were blessed to be expecting again. Believe me, I was stunned at how quickly Tracy-Ann made her decision. It wasn't planned until it was - in the moment.

Naturally we did our research and utilized a new obstetrician. Everything was different this time around. From the ultrasound to the blood tests that went unchecked before, we were better prepared for what was to come.

Ironically, she cleared the first trimester around the same time our twins would have been born. This time, however, we did not tell any of our family members. We were very cautious. God had a plan for us, and we know it was His will that we experienced such a loss. He was preparing us for our miracle.

Having a child is an incredible blessing. Trey's subsequent diagnosis did not change that. I learned that Autism is not a death sentence. It is a time to be present more than ever, not to remove yourself from the journey. It is ok to be disappointed, hurt, even angry, for we are human. It is not ok to be consumed by those feelings to the point you ignore what needs to be done to help your child.

We already have stereotypes stacked against us as Black men. We are told that we are not involved, we are deadbeats, although there is overwhelming evidence to the contrary.

I allowed denial to be a hindrance. Although I did not know about Autism or any of the signs or symptoms, my wife did. I let foolish pride keep me from listening to her instincts and acknowledging the truth. Writing is my therapy, and I am no longer ashamed to say that I failed my son. It was my inaction that delayed his diagnosis. It is a reality I still deal with.

The great thing about God is that He makes no mistakes, and He allows us the ability to make things right.

Tracy-Ann says you must mourn the child you thought you were going to have. Such a powerful statement. I had to give up my preconceived notions of who I thought my son would be and realize God gave us someone greater. Speaking for myself, I found purpose in advocating for Autism awareness and acceptance because children on the spectrum deserve to be treated like their peers who are not.

We are not perfect but let us not be selfish. It takes nothing to test and rule out a disability. Doing nothing at all is the same as abandoning that child when he/she needs you the most. That's what I did for years. Realizing I was repeating what happened in my past, I chose to be the father who stayed in the fight to help Trey find his voice.

This is my testimony.

SIGNS

When Trey was born, he did not speak to us immediately. The cry we expected to hear was delayed momentarily. Since he was Frankenstein breech, which meant he was upside down in the womb, Tracy-Ann needed a Caesarean section to bring him into the world. She was laid out on a table in the delivery room separated by a blue sheet right above her belly. I sat down next to her oblivious to what was happening on the other side. We heard the doctor announce his arrival, but there was no sound.

My wife started to panic. Was this history repeating itself? Once again there was no response from a physician, just the look we saw 11 months earlier. They brought Trey to our side of the partition to see him for the first time. We saw a pink baby looking back at us with what looked like jet-black eyes.

"Why is he not crying?" Tracy-Ann wondered aloud.

The nurse holding Trey immediately whisked him over to a small table next to a scale. She proceeded to use a suction tube to clear the mucous from his nose and mouth. Once his nasal and oral passages were free, he spoke to us.

I could not stop staring at him. I felt the urge to speak to him in a high-pitched tone normally reserved for things we consider to be cute. As soon as the nurse inquired why I wasn't taking pictures, I quickly turned into the paparazzi. I snapped pictures of our boy on the scale, getting his hands and feet inked and printed, the nurse held him up for me to take more shots. I still remember his bottom lip dropping down in a sad pout ready to cry. I always get emotional thinking about how much in love I was with my son at that moment.

When he met his mother for the first time laying on her chest, it was amazing how at peace he was. He stopped crying immediately, his eyes covered with ointment and blinking slowly, when placed on her cozy bosom. I have a picture of that as well.

For the next four days, as Tracy-Ann recovered, I made regular trips to the nursery just to look at Trey. I would speak to him when I saw his eyes were open, I would stare at him when his eyes were closed. Whenever I was away from him, I would listen to hear his cry. I was obsessed. I learned to swaddle him in the customary white blanket with the green and red stripes provided by the hospital. Anything I could do just to look at him, I did. I had the son I dreamed about. The boy that would carry on my name. The heir to the throne. My legacy personified. It was not about me anymore. I had a little one who would look to me for guidance, as his teacher, his hero. It was a huge responsibility. I wondered if this was how my Dad felt when I was born. I used to keep a photo of myself, just days old, light-skinned with pink lips, my right eye slightly open peeking out at my surroundings. Trey looked just like me.

When my wife was finally discharged, I was hands-on with everything. I placed Trey in his car seat, I looked at him as I carried him the distance from the hospital to my car. I made sure the car seat was buckled in properly and that he was secure. I could not see his face during the drive home because of the rear-facing car seat. That was the longest hour ever!

Tracy-Ann and I were married for almost two years at this time and living in our third apartment, of no fault of our own. As new parents we wanted to make sure we provided the safest possible environment for Trey. The place we resided in when we welcomed him home for the first time was not perfect by any stretch of the imagination, but we made it work.

Before his arrival we made sure his room was prepared with the finest baby furniture and accessories courtesy of Babies R' Us: a crib made of mahogany wood, a matching changing table, multiple packs of diapers, milk, pacifiers, blankets, baby toys, and skin care products. This was our first born and we were not playing around.

I also did not know what I was doing. I was learning on the fly as is customary when taking on something new. This "new" was a human being. Even though Tracy-Ann had experience with babies from raising her younger cousins, I was responsible for a whole new life without the benefit of an instruction manual. We went to great lengths to take care of Trey, going out of our way to make sure he had everything we did not. If you look at pictures from when he was a baby, we put his wardrobe on par with any celebrity infant: all the Air Jordan sneakers I never had, velvet tracksuits, and sheepskin coats.

Trey knew he was loved. We doted on him at every turn. He always knew when the camera was on him. He was always smiling.

He was also a babbling baby who was hitting all his milestones. One of my favorite videos that I can't find is that of me singing happy birthday to my mother. He was a little over ten months old at the time. I repeatedly sang to him "Happy birthday to Nana." After the third repetition, he began to sing the same refrain.

"Happy birthday to Nana! Happy birthday to Nana!"

I vividly recall holding him in my arms shocked that he was repeating what I was saying. Of course, you never capture the initial action on film so I did what any newly minted, excited Dad would do: I put him down in his crib, pulled out my camera, set it to 'video' and started singing "Happy Birthday to Nana!" praying that he would say it again.

When he did, I could not contain my excitement. He was so small, and his smile was a mile wide. He was so happy that he was getting such a reaction out of me.

Everything wasn't always positive. As with any relationship, there were some challenges. We were prepared for our baby to get sick, or so we thought. Not every infant can speak like the character 'Boss Baby'. If that were so, parents all over the world would have an easier time tending to their child's needs.

Trey cried a lot. The trick was trying to discern what type of cry it was. I was only familiar with the 'hunger cry' from watching television shows and movies, something that can be remedied with a warm bottle. That led to the 'gas cry', a sound that would not be quelled until he was burped.

There were times when feeding and burping Trey would not stop him from crying. In those instances where we did not know the cause of his distress it was an immediate trip to the emergency room. His momma did not play around. Where my approach was more of the home remedy, wait-and-see variety, she was ready to go to the ER at the slightest sign of trouble. She was of the mindset that it was better to be safe than sorry.

We wanted to make sure Trey would be safeguarded from any illnesses. We brought him to a pediatrician to receive his immunization shots, simple preventative measures to ensure his health and safety. He would receive multiple injections at the same time, among them the measles, mumps, and rubella (MMR) shots. He cried out as the needles pierced his skin, nothing out of the ordinary. It was during the ride home and for the rest of the evening we noticed he continued to cry and was very fussy. We figured the sting of the needles was the cause of his irritability.

Over the next few days Trey was running a fever that would break and repeatedly come back. As I recall, most of his visits to the hospital in the weeks that followed were caused by an ear infection. I've had ear infections as a child. I remember the pain very well. I couldn't imagine an infant repeatedly dealing with that discomfort, but Trey did. We were at a loss as to what was causing these infections. We brought him to his pediatrician who repeatedly assured us he was fine.

In the weeks that followed, we noticed Trey was different. He no longer spoke to us. He wasn't laughing. The happy baby that sang to his Nana had disappeared. I didn't see the joy in his face, just a blank stare. I remember Tracy-Ann saying that he looked different. His eating habits changed. He began to smell his food and look at it. He would run it through his fingers as if it was putty. He was crying all the time and it was difficult to comfort him. He wasn't responding to his name. I saw the despair in my wife's face because we could not explain what was happening to him.

These were major red flags that I did not investigate believing that as he got older, he would begin formulating words. He didn't have an issue running around the house, so I thought he was ok. I refused to act on the signs.

One afternoon he was running in the living room area. This would not usually be alarming because our living room had carpet and it was a space that was relatively open save for a wall unit that was off to the left. There were three separate pieces. The two endpieces kept our fine china (plates, teacups, and silverware gifted from our wedding) and the massive centerpiece housed our 42" television (considered huge at the time) and other parts of our entertainment system.

As Trey was running back and forth, I stayed close to him, but further than arm's length as he was old enough where he did not have an issue with balance. As he turned in the direction of the wall unit, he took a couple of steps and tripped on the carpet. His momentum took him forward, further than expected. His body hit the carpet, but he kept going. It was like watching a ripple wave of dominoes falling. They say the head is the heaviest part of the human body and Trey had a huge one for his age. We always joked he would be very smart by default. In this instance it worked to his disadvantage as his face hit the edge of the wall unit.

I did not expect him to land at that spot based on where he started his fall. It happened so fast I was unable to react, but I remember it in slow motion. I ran over to pick him up fearing the worst because the sound of the impact would make a grown man cry, let alone a baby. To my surprise he popped right back up, but he was not crying, he was laughing. The sound was weird. It wasn't the kind of laughter I heard when I made a funny face in front of him. He was in shock, and I was stunned at his response.

I picked him up and saw a line of blood fall from above his left eye and I immediately panicked. He was still laughing as the blood streamed down his face. I'm not sure if he was delirious, but out of all the emotions to come from an accident that drew blood, laughter is not what I expected.

At this point I am frantically pulling paper towels and pressing it on his head to stop the blood, praying it is just a cut. The wound would not stop bleeding, the first troubling sign. The second sign was when I finally got to see it up close without the blood, I noticed the skin was broken. His eyebrow looked the same as the right side of my mouth when I got hit with a block of ice during a snowball fight in the seventh grade. I needed stitches to close that wound.

I became very nervous at that point because it would mean a trip to the emergency room. I could not see them pulling a needle through his eyebrow at such a young age. He was still not crying at this point, but I was ready to have a breakdown.

I not only had to worry about the open wound, but the impact to Trey's head. I had to keep him from falling asleep for the next few hours. In a Caribbean family, any blow to the head meant drinking something sweet. I guess the sugar rush helped to keep the person awake. I put a band-aid on the cut as a temporary fix. Tracy-Ann was more panicked than upset when I told her what happened. She didn't see the accident occur so trying to explain to her over the phone was an exercise in futility.

Surprisingly we never went to the emergency room. Tracy-Ann contacted her Aunt Gertrude, who was a nurse, to explain what happened and ask for advice on where to bring Trey for medical attention. I remember Aunt Gertrude being so calm stating that she could stitch him up on her own. I was confused. I never knew an open wound could be closed without a needle, but when she stopped by, like an unsung hero, she basically saved me. Even though I didn't cause his accident, Trey still fell on my watch, with no witnesses to boot. I felt responsible and blamed myself for not preventing it although, from where I was standing, I would've had to be Superman to catch him from falling.

I watched closely as Trey was laid across Aunt Gertrude's lap. He looked worried, eyes darting quickly from her face to her hands. I was nervous for him, my anxiety heightened with anticipation. I was charged with the task of holding his arms so he would not move. I knew whatever she was about to do would cause him some discomfort. When I grabbed his arms, I saw the panic in his eyes as they moved from me to Aunt Gertrude. He put up as much of a resistance as a one-and-a-half-year-old could against an adult holding his arms and legs.

Aunt Gertrude put on white latex gloves and pulled out a clear gel-like substance with her right hand. With her left thumb and index fingers she squeezed the open cut on his eyebrow together to close the wound. I don't know if it was the pressure of her holding his eyebrow, but Trey began to cry immediately. Go figure. The head to wall unit impact made him laugh, but the process of the wound closure got the reaction I expected from the fall.

With her right hand, Aunt Gertrude spread the clear substance across Trey's eyebrow where her two fingers were holding the skin together. His screams were almost unbearable, but I had to keep him steady while the substance dried. Days later, once the substance dissolved, all that was left was a light brown line in the middle of his eyebrow. This was my introduction to adhesive stitches. I was truly indebted to Aunt Gertrude.

Reflecting on that day, his reaction to being wounded was inappropriate. That was another sign I should have followed up on. I can say I was in a state of denial that kept me in a constant fear of the unknown. I was listening to the narrative of what family members were saying to Tracy-Ann when she shared her concerns: he just needed prayer, he was still a baby, and he would grow out of whatever it was.

JANUARY 2009.

A few months after Trey's injury, we were on the move again. The space we were departing was not suitable for raising a child. It was frustrating because we were overpaying for living conditions that became woefully unsanitary.

Trey would turn two in March. Suffice it to say there wasn't any evidence of the "terrible two's" anywhere. It was quite the opposite, in fact. He was very quiet and respectful of adults. He was always smiling. When he wasn't it was the only way we knew something was wrong. A major milestone moment was in the fall of 2009: his first day of school.

We found a private school only blocks away, that was not a daycare, that taught kids his age. At the age of two I was still in the highchair watching episodes of "Happy Days" and "Sesame Street" at my babysitter's house. There was no such thing as pre-K

2 or pre-K 3 when I was growing up. It was nursery school until you were four and then you began pre-kindergarten.

SEPTEMBER 8, 2009.

I remember Trey's first day like it was yesterday. He had a freshly shaved head (we decided to shave off his cornrows), an orange Roc-a-Wear short-sleeved shirt, khaki shorts, and black sneakers. I remember him being so happy, far from the anxiety and first day jitters I expected. Did he even know where he was going? I ran down the steps to capture the moment on camera of him walking out the door. He gave me a big smile as his Mom held his hand. When we arrived at the school, we met the principal and made our way to the classroom.

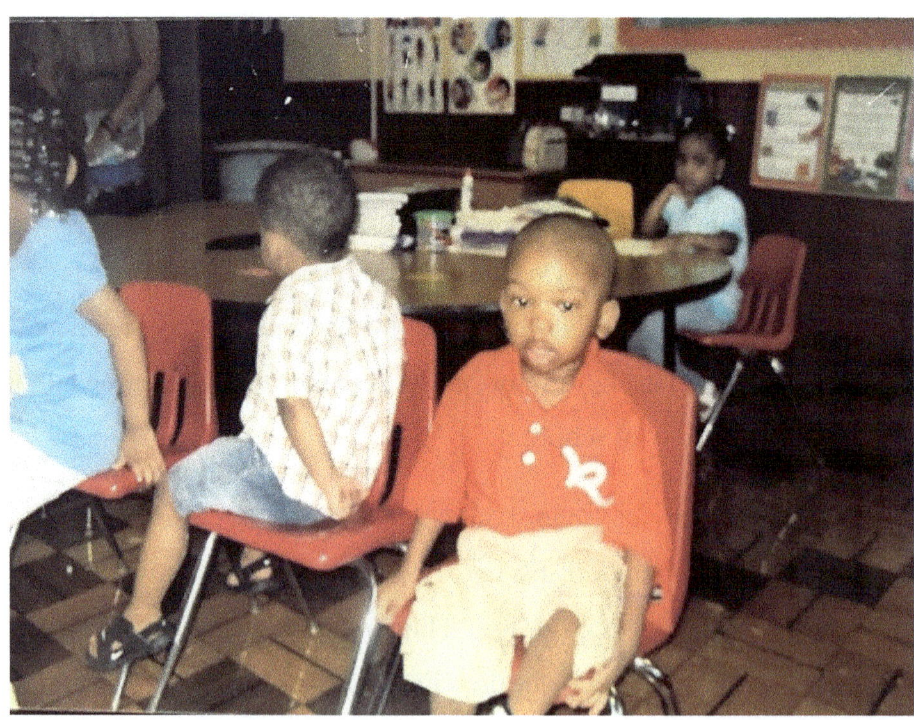

Trey's teacher was a lady named Ms. McRae. She welcomed us to the school and focused her attention immediately on him. He did not react to her greeting. There were other kids already in the classroom. Small red chairs were placed around a table. Each child chose a seat. I walked Trey around to the next available chair and sat him down.

My wife and I expected some sort of reaction from our son, but, surprisingly, he did not cry. He did look a little nervous as he realized we were in a place he did not recognize. I took a picture of him sitting in the chair. He was not smiling this time. Tracy-Ann stood by the door for her own sanity. She hated that she would have to leave her baby in the care of a stranger.

I kissed Trey on his head and said my goodbye. As he watched me walk away, his expression remained stoic. He did not jump off the chair and run after me. There was no first day separation anxiety. It was so weird. Tracy-Ann, on the other hand, needed multiple tissues.

This was a milestone moment leaving your child in the care of an educator. I believe teachers are an extension of the parents and finding the appropriate school setting for a child is one of the most important decisions you can make. It is a whole new world for a child, where they will get to learn new things, interact with other kids, and make new friends.

The next day when we dropped Trey at school, he cried, he

screamed, he yelled when he saw us walking away to leave him. This was the response we were expecting on day one. What was a smooth departure yesterday, became difficult on this day. I thought nothing of the delayed reaction. His meltdown made me feel bad about leaving him. This time it was my wife who was urging **me** to exit the room. With added reassurance from Ms. McRae, I did just that.

I was mainly tasked with picking Trey up from school in the afternoon. Thankfully, I saw no evidence that he did not want to be in the class. As the year went on his teacher shared his progress, he was able to point out the letters hanging from the ceiling when I called them out. There were a few times I noticed him playing by himself. Where other kids were sitting around the table and interacting with each other, Trey was in the play area or sitting at the same table but away from the group. I did not think anything of this because Ms. McRae would give such a glowing report about the day he had.

I was also distracted by the three little girls who, when I arrived to pick him up, would jump out of their seat and run to help Trey get ready. One little girl would grab his jacket and put it on for him, another would grab his bookbag and help him put it on, and the third child would grab his lunchbox. I thought this was so amusing I did not stop to think that maybe they were helping Trey because he did not know how to help himself. I was completely missing the signs playing out right in front of my face.

HOME

He was only three years old, yet the teacher made Trey out to be this monster of a child. Just a month into the beginning of pre-K3, his behavior was different. He let us know he did not want to go to school in not-so-subtle ways. He spoke to us through his actions. The kicking and crying before we left the house only intensified as I arrived at the school building. This wasn't the normal anxiety. He had no problem going to Ms. McRae's class the year before.

There was a time that I remember going to pick Trey up at the end of the school day and when I arrived at the classroom he was moving around back and forth. He had a smile on his face, but the teacher did not seem so happy. She looked stressed and frustrated. When I asked how Trey was, she took a deep breath, giving herself time to sanitize her response. Although she gave me a straight answer, her words were most definitely chosen carefully. She told me Trey would not stay seated for long periods of time, he distracted the other kids, and she had to constantly redirect him to his seat.

I could not believe how aggravated the teacher was. The boy is three years old. I was immediately put off by her attitude. Trying to educate a room full of little ones is not easy, however this teacher was really complaining. I didn't hear this from Ms. McRae. It takes a certain temperament to work with young children and this teacher came across as impatient. I could only imagine what she was saying or doing to Trey during the school day. I understood why he was apprehensive. Since there was no other preK-3 class in the building it was not long before we removed him from the school entirely.

This would be a huge undertaking. There are parents who send their children to school every day for the sole purpose of gaining some alone time to relax or recuperate. Here we were doing the exact opposite, but not for lack of trying. We searched for other private schools in the area to enroll Trey in, but since the school year was already underway there were no private schools with an opening for new students. Around this time, I was making up for lost income after being laid off from the hotel I worked at. I was receiving unemployment assistance for a few months before landing a job at another hotel working the overnight shift as a Front Desk supervisor. I was given an hour break for lunch, time I used to take a nap. I knew with an infant at home, I wasn't going to get much sleep during the day.

Tracy-Ann had already returned to work full-time from her maternity leave earlier than she would have liked because we needed the extra money. It was ultimately agreed upon that since she worked during the day, I would be home to watch and take care of Trey. It was either that or leave him in a classroom where he would be verbally abused, and God knows what else.

Although we agreed on this plan to remove Trey, we underestimated how difficult it would be to find another school for him. We believed this would be a temporary arrangement that would last up to a month at the latest. We visited so many schools in the interim and none had space for a new student.

There were plenty of times when my body clock, completely thrown out of whack, would remind my brain and ultimately my eyes that I needed rest, but I had my personal alarm clock in the form of crying to wake me up. When I agreed to watch Trey, I did not consider how active he would be.

He was not the same child who was using our sofa to pull himself up, who could not put one leg in front of the other and keep his balance for an extended period, who used the hallway from our bedroom to the living room as his personal runway, looking like he was walking a tightrope over a ravine of ravenous alligators. He was walking on his own. He was a runner. He was not going to stay still because I wanted to rest. That was not his problem.

Suddenly those little naps I tried to steal when I got home from work, and he was still asleep, became few and far between. When Trey slept, I would make sure there were barriers between him and the sides of the bed so he would not roll off. The biggest barrier was me. Soon enough I was not an obstacle anymore.

I began to feel something crawl over me and I would sit up and grab him. He was trying to get out of the room. Maybe he was tired of hearing me snore, I don't know, but he wanted to be anywhere but next to me. Trey was smart. If I wanted to know if his brain was developing, I needed to look no further than the ways he tried to get out of our bedroom. He would slide off the bed from the bottom so as not to wake me up but would meet another roadblock in the form of our bedroom door.

I would not always be alert to catch him. I remember jumping up out of my sleep and Trey was nowhere in the bedroom. I was dumfounded as to how he was able to get past me, but I couldn't dwell on it for too long. The bedroom door was open. The speed at which I hopped out of bed could not be understated. There was another bedroom to the immediate left. He was not in there. I ran into the bathroom in the hallway. He was not there. The next stop was the kitchen.

With each room of the house checked the thought ran through my mind of what I would do if I found him in any of these areas. I mean, there were real dangers in each room, especially for small children. Compound that with the fact that he was not making it easy for me to find him. I thought I could count on a child that was three years old to speak to me when I called his name, but he was quiet. Too quiet.

While I appreciate Trey wanting to allow me to heal my body by getting some much-needed sleep, he failed to realize that if I was sleeping, I could not watch what he was doing. Obviously, he was too young to consciously make this decision for me. Or maybe he did realize it. I knew one thing I was lucky he couldn't talk yet because I did not need his mom knowing that he was walking around the house while I was asleep.

My wife still had a way of knowing what was going on even if she wasn't present. I rarely believed in the woman's intuition stuff, but I was definitely a believer in Tracy-Ann's power to see. If she wasn't physically in the room, she would see my frantic attempts to locate our son in her dreams. Her grandmother lived with us, something that was non-negotiable. Her grandma practically raised her as a child. Needless to say, grandma was very influential in her life.

Grandma was a flowing river of knowledge and wisdom gained from a life well lived. Truthfully, I was fortunate that she was in the house for more reasons than one. She ended up watching Trey when I wasn't. That is exactly where he was that morning. I looked everywhere but grandma's room for obvious reasons: I did not want to let her know I had lost the boy, but he already told on me by showing up without me. Which is how I thought Tracy-Ann discovered I was struggling to keep up with him.

When we agreed that I would take on the responsibility of caring for Trey during the day, I made the case that fatigue would not be a factor. I did not want to pass off watching my own child to someone else. If I was home, I could surely look after my son. I really had to convince her that I was fit for the responsibility. She had reservations that I would be too tired to effectively supervise him. She believed my body would shut down.

Even if I knew she was right, what was the alternative? We did not want a stranger coming into our home to babysit. My mom lived a few blocks away, but she worked during the day, same with Tracy-Ann's mom.

That would leave grandma. I did not want to put that burden on her. She had watched enough grandchildren and other people's children to last a lifetime. She had a special love for Trey, however. She would do anything for him. Regardless of what I was doing grandma would make sure she kept an eye on him. She was the backup I didn't know I had. Still, she was relaying everything she saw to Tracy-Ann. She had to be. How else could I explain why my wife would come at me questioning my ability to look after him?

"You're tired Jamiyl," she would say. "Are you sure you can watch Trey? You need rest." What my wife was doing was trying to give me a way out. Her gut was telling her that I could not do this alone, but she needed to hear me say it. I already had it in my head that since I took on the responsibility to watch Trey during the day, that any evidence that I could not do so was a sign of weakness. I figured she knew about me losing track of him and was trying to undermine me.

Stubborn pride and ego, mixed with anger at being called out made me more defiant. I had to prove that as a man I did not need any help. I became aggravated with her at simple questions, defensive in my tone as I reassured her that I was fine. That one day was an aberration. She kept telling me that having a child was not about self. I did not understand what she was saying. Not admitting I needed help was a selfish act. I had a false sense of what I was capable of under the circumstances.

A typical day with Trey involved getting him cleaned up and out of his night clothes. Then I would make sure he got something to eat for breakfast. He was a very picky eater. I don't know if it was because he was so eager to move around. The only time he stayed still was when I put him in his highchair, or he was watching television. I had to find creative ways to get him to eat.

When I had finished preparing the food I would yell out "food time!" and Trey would repeat what I said. I assumed he was excited to eat. And he probably was, just not what I was giving him. Whatever I put in front of him, he had to smell it. Whether it be hot cereal, cold cereal with milk, boiled or scrambled eggs, it was like pulling teeth trying to get the boy to eat. When all else failed, Pediasure saved the day.

Lunchtime was more of the same struggle. Chef Boyardee spaghetti was hit or miss depending on the day. Usually, ravioli or lasagna would pass the sniff test. I knew I had to make sure he was fed because the first question from Tracy-Ann when she got home would be about his food intake. It seemed like whatever I answered was not enough. "That's all?" or "What else?" was a common response. I tried my best, but it was hard to feed a child who wouldn't eat.

Trey loved snacks. I thought a steady diet of apple sauce, Cheeze-it, yogurt, and Capri-Sun would suffice, but I was quickly told that was not real food. Pediasure bottles were soon added to the list. I turned to Lunchables and macaroni & cheese to some degree of success. The pressing issue was figuring out a way to stay awake in between breakfast and lunch.

I needed to find something to keep me awake and, in the past, for me it was video games. The NBA 2K series was a go-to favorite of mine. I would turn on Trey's favorite show on Nickelodeon Jr. and fire up my Xbox 360 and play. I did not speak to him.

He would be so enamored with shows like '*Barney*', '*Yo Gabba Gabba*', and '*Wow Wow Wubbzy!*' that he would not move from in front of the television. He would stand so close I had to constantly tell him to move back, but he would always find himself a foot away from the screen with his head tilted slightly back taking in everything – until I changed the channel.

I had those old silver 42-inch Sony televisions when they were all the rage back in the early to mid-aughts. The six-disc DVD player was connected to what was considered the big screen. That meant whenever I wanted to watch live television after hours of kids shows, I had to press the input button on the remote control. The screen would fill with rice grains as I passed each input category. Trey took off running like he saw a ghost. I never seen him move so fast. He would eventually peek around the corner to see if the picture was back on the television. I did not understand why this scared him so much. He was way too young to know about the movie Poltergeist.

There was another occasion when I was changing the inputs and a loud noise emanated from the speakers. It was like a feedback noise when speakers pop. The noise was unexpected and scared me so you could guess what it did to Trey. This time he ran off with his hands covering his ears. It got to a point that whenever he knew I was changing from DVD player to live television he would be around the corner and in the hallway before I could push a button. I never told Tracy-Ann at the time about this. Maybe I would have gained some clarity about what was really happening.

The running out of the room should have been another red flag. I was unaware that Trey was having a sensory reaction.

Tracy-Ann's grandma would walk out periodically to see what was going on. I thought I was in good shape because I was awake, and, although I wasn't speaking to him, Trey was occupied. Later that evening I would be asked about the activities I did with him. I thought it was another subtle attack on my ability to supervise. I just knew grandma was telling her I was playing video games. I truly did not see what the problem was. I was alert and Trey was watching his favorite shows.

Unbeknownst to me, my wife was using her social work training to assess Trey. She was building her evidence to corroborate her gut feeling. She was counting on me to do more academic work with him to compensate for his being out of school, but I was too consumed with finishing a season in 2K, under the guise of finding a way to stay awake, to realize that I needed to engage with Trey more. I needed to speak to him.

I was supposed to be his teacher in the interim. Tracy-Ann was leaving books for Trey to read and math worksheets for me to go over with him. I would skim through the math, and I would read the picture books to him, but nothing with the consistency of a daily lesson plan. I truly believed that children learn by being placed in situations. I did not recall my babysitter speaking to me all day.

I failed to realize it was not about me. My responsibility was to make sure Trey was being mentally stimulated and I was negligent. When I was pressed for a progress report, I felt nothing I did was enough. I wasn't getting credit for the time I did spend working with him. I was fooling myself. The days I put Trey in front of the television far outnumbered the days I taught him. I was being lazy. My anger was misdirected at my wife when I should have been mad with myself for not being upfront about my struggles to stay awake. I should have been thankful that grandma was there when I wasn't. It was easier for me to blame an elderly woman for 'exposing' me than admit to myself that I was giving her all the ammunition by failing my son in real time.

It turns out that it was grandma who was feeding Trey in the mornings whenever I was sleeping. While he was a picky eater, on some days he was also working on a stomach full of porridge or hot cereal by the time I woke up. The times I would lock my bedroom door to keep Trey from running out the room if he woke up before me, I was hurting him. I was keeping grandma from feeding him. I learned that grandma refused to share anything that was happening because she did not want to come between Tracy-Ann and myself. Years later I learned it was her mother that told what was happening.

I remember my mother-in-law came to visit periodically and would spend the night at times. Grandma was telling her what she didn't want to tell my wife. My immaturity had me pointing fingers at the wrong person. I was not honest from the beginning. There was nothing wrong with me going to work at night, but I was underestimating the effect on my body. The fatigue I felt during the day hindered me from being an active father to Trey in every sense. He deserved better. If I would have taken the time to communicate with him, I would have known that he had an issue speaking to me.

At that point I was destroying my marriage. I had broken my wife's trust by not being honest with her. She was fed up with my attitude towards her for asking simple questions. She depended on me to watch Trey, to engage him in conversation, to consistently teach him, but I was not doing so. She advised me that I was endangering the welfare of our child and being in the field she worked in she could not stand by and allow it to happen. Hearing that she thought I was putting our child in danger infuriated me. I pushed back. I didn't want to believe I was harming my son. She was at her wit's end with my attitude and the financial issues we were having. She was overwhelmed by my lack of support for her feeling that something was wrong with our son. I did not know how close she was to leaving with him.

RECONNECTION

In the midst of the turmoil I was facing in my marriage, I remember the promise I made to myself that I would always be a voice for my son and I would never walk out on my family. I was breaking that promise by not speaking to him, and I was in danger of my wife walking out on **me**. Despite the struggles we were experiencing I was going to fight. His birthday was coming up. A perfect time to show my worthiness.

I came from a broken family. In many ways I was still the ten-year-old my father walked out on because I had no idea how to handle crisis. I was disappointed with myself for not being able to alleviate the financial responsibilities from my wife. I was not being a good husband and I was being told I was not being a good father. It was important for me to break that generational curse and be better than my Dad had ever been to me, but I was failing.

My Dad inspired me two-fold. He showed me the unconditional love of a father to son on one hand, and on the other, showed me the negative impact of absenteeism. I wanted to break the cycle of hurt his abandonment caused. I wanted to be a better father to my son simply by being there. I did not have a male role model during my formative teenage years, when I needed guidance. I knew I had to forgive him to be the father Trey deserved. Trey was turning four and a meeting was way overdue. I decided I would not be the reason they did not know each other.

MARCH 12, 2011.

We celebrated Trey's 4th birthday at Chuck E. Cheese in Long Island. I invited my Dad to the party and, to my surprise, he showed up bearing gifts. After so much time apart I was still learning to reopen my heart to a relationship I had given up on years ago.

When my Dad showed up, the party was well underway, and we had already started serving the food. I watched him say his pleasantries to everyone and make a beeline to Trey. He lifted my son off his feet and stared at him. For a moment I wondered if he was reminiscing about me at that age. I thought about the gravity of moment: three generations of Samuels men finally in the same room together. It was beautiful to see.

A couple of months later I was shocked to get a call from him asking for my home address. He still lived in Queens, but he was going to travel to Brooklyn to see me. The irony of how simple this seemed was not lost on me, for he was only a borough away all those years ago.

Since our reunion in 2004, my dad and I had two false starts, but this felt real. I really wanted to keep in contact with him. He was showing up for Trey and it did not feel forced. I wanted my son to know his grandfather, so this was a dream come true. He showed up at my door with a neon green plastic big wheel tricycle toy. I was confused, until I realized it was a video game system. There were input wires to connect to the television. Once the system was powered on, the driving game appeared. I put Trey in the seat, and he immediately started turning the steering wheel.

I appreciated the effort, but a part of me knew it was on account of Trey. Although I was happy my Dad was going to great lengths for his grandson, a part of me felt a little weird. Call me selfish, but he had my phone number prior to Chuck E. Cheese and never went out of his way to find me like this. Personal feelings aside, I was encouraged. This was a great first step in building back my trust that we would have a consistent relationship.

OCTOBER 2011.

I saw my Dad's number on my ringing cellphone. I looked at Tracy-Ann, who was sitting directly next to me, when I answered. One of the first things he asked was if I was taking care of her. We were both stunned. It was the first time anyone in my family held me accountable for how I was treating my wife. In that moment it was important for him to know that I was taking care of my responsibilities as a man. I wanted to scream 'you never showed me how!' I was left to learn from my wife what she expected from me. I was embarrassed that I had to be trained on things I should have known already.

I thought about what if I had sought him out as a teenager instead of running and hiding in the park when I knew he was at my aunt's house. What if we had an actual conversation that day in 2004, merely two months after my engagement and cleared the air about his decision to leave? What if that conversation opened the door to further dialogue and he was able to give me advice about what to expect when getting married? How having a wife is different than a girlfriend? How to prepare for being a husband? How had he felt as a first-time father at 25 years of age? By simply asking Tracy-Ann that question, I knew I could have learned so much if we had the time together.

This call was not only about my ability to care for my wife. After letting him know we were expecting another child, my Dad informed us that he had been diagnosed with cancer. It was a punch to the gut I did not expect. He would pass away six months later. As I was just getting reacquainted with him, my Dad was gone again. I not only lost him a second time, but Trey would also never get to truly know his grandfather.

BACK TO SCHOOL

SEPTEMBER 6, 2011.

We knew we were not sending Trey back to the previous school. Thankfully, we were able to find another private school a couple of blocks away. This school was in a building that appeared to be a church. It was a plus that religion would be a major part of the program.

Trey seemed happy in his new surroundings. By the end of the first week, he was able to tell us the name of his teacher: Ms. Kane*. I noticed that a lot of Trey's responses were one-word answers. He often mimicked what he heard on television. At one point, a large portion of his speech was dialogue from shows like '*Little Einsteins*', '*Wonder Pets*', and '*Backyardigans*'. I had never seen anything like it.

Tracy-Ann called it echolalia. I saw the influence of our summer spent not speaking to him consistently and it wasn't pretty. I finally realized why she was so angry with me. Still, I believed if he was placed around other kids, he would form a natural bond and conversation would follow. I was determined to make sure this school was right for him.

By the second week, Trey was able to tell us the names of some of his classmates. I felt he would be able to make new friends in this setting. Around this time, I noticed his budding love for music. Any time he heard a song he liked he would rock from side to side. This was different. A few months prior we bought a plastic drum set for Christmas. We played a song on the radio, and, to our surprise, he played the drums right on key. Exciting as this was at the time it did not dawn on me that he had a gift.

Trey also had a great singing voice. He would sing at random, mainly religious songs. One morning he walked up to the ironing board and began touching it with his fingers as if he was playing the piano. He sang as he played his imaginary instrument. I wondered where he learned these songs.

One morning I took Trey to school and stayed to see how he was doing. At a certain time of the morning the kids would all line up and file out of their classrooms into an open space where there were seven to eight rows of chairs lined up for the kids to sit on.

A wooden piano sat at the front of the room to the left a few feet away from the chairs. At 9 o'clock, children began walking out of their classrooms led by their teachers and filling in the seats in age order. The two-year old kids in the first two rows, the three-year old kids behind them, and so on. It seemed that Trey paid close attention to this set up and committed it to memory.

This gathering was a daily routine at the school called "chapel".

It was reminiscent of a church service where the teachers led the children in songs and passages from the Bible. Before chapel began, an older man with glasses dressed in a suit and tie sat on a small wooden stool in front of the piano and began to play. I looked at Trey when the music began and saw a child fascinated by the way the man was moving his fingers across the keys. I noticed as the children sang, he knew every single word. These were the songs I was hearing in the house. To my dismay what I thought to be natural, flowing speech was him repeating what he was hearing.

After chapel was over the kids returned to their classrooms for the lessons of the day. I took this opportunity to ask Ms. Kane how Trey was doing in class.

"Let me show you some of his work," she said running her thumb through a pile of folders.

Once she arrived at Trey's name, she pulled the folder out.

"I have no problem with Trey in regard to his behavior," she continued pulling her glasses slightly down to look at me.

"He is quiet," she continued. "He needs to participate more in class."

Ms. Kane opened the folder and pulled out a picture of a farm. There was a barn in the background. In the foreground was a picture of a pig in mud, on the opposite side were a group of chickens, and a cow near the barn with its head in the grass.

"I ask all the students to color a picture just to see where their skill level is," Ms. Kane said as she handed me the picture.

The entire page was colored in blue crayon outside of the lines. I did not know what to think about what I was seeing. Ms. Kane showed me the same picture from a different student. A different color was used to represent each animal and the surrounding scenery.

"There is one child that sits directly across from Trey," she began. "He says Trey is always bothering him."

The comment caught me off guard. I had never heard a complaint about Trey regarding his behavior with other kids. I needed more details.

"Does the child talk to Trey?" I asked.

"Yes, however, no matter what the child says Trey only smiles in return," offered Ms. Kane. "He thinks Trey is laughing at him."

In my mind I was expecting something heinous, more aggravating in nature. Trey was a happy child. How could someone get upset about a kid smiling at them? It seemed like nothing, but the teacher thought it important enough an issue to bring to my attention.

I went home and shared this information with Tracy-Ann. All of Trey's teachers were saying the same thing about his lack of communication in school. Was this a cause for concern at his age?

I was shy as a child. I didn't really start speaking in class until the second grade. I just thought he was following in my footsteps. Kids usually fashion themselves in the image of their parents.

Tracy-Ann's instincts told her something different. She mentioned that the way Trey colored was not appropriate. But he was still very young. She also thought there was an issue with the repetition in his speech. Shy or not, at his age he should be speaking in full sentences, at least around his immediate family. He was the most comfortable around us. We could not get more than a couple of words out of him at a time. Although I believed his speech would be better in a classroom setting around other kids, I was concerned enough to question Ms. Kane every single day I picked Trey up from school.

Whenever I would ask how Trey was during the day, I would get vague hand gestures and contorted facial expressions. I wasn't asking for a book report. A simple "he was ok" or "he spoke today" would suffice. At least an update on the case of the boy who was bothered by Trey smiling at him. I noticed Trey remained at the same table. I came expecting a progress report and I got nothing of substance. It got to the point where I wanted to ask if Ms. Kane was in the classroom the entire day, or did she step out as soon as the parents left the school and never came back until right before dismissal. How do you not have anything to say about my child after being so willing to let me know that he could not color properly?

At that point I knew I could not trust Ms. Kane. She was not revealing anything about Trey's time in the classroom. I devised a plan to gain access to the school during the day to keep an eye on him. I took the opportunity to meet with the school's principal to request if I could do my internship for a course I was taking to become a certified teacher's assistant in the kindergarten class.

I did not place myself directly in Trey's class to avoid any conflict of interest, but I let Ms. Kane know that I would be in the building on a regular basis in the classroom right next door. I spent the next couple of months assisting the kindergarten teacher and keeping an eye on Trey. I began to pay closer attention to more of his behaviors I once thought were cute.

When he got excited, he usually jumped around, smiling, and flapping his right arm by his ear. I noticed these hand movements when he was trying to speak. I knew he should have been putting words together by now, but his lack of verbal communication was not the only sign I started to recognize. I watched how he was putting on his clothes. He would put his undershirt on backwards, he could not button his pants, or put on a jacket by himself.

I also noticed that for Trey everything had to be the same all the time. His toys, especially his cars, had to be aligned just right. His books had to be stacked in a straight pile without a corner turned in a different direction. The tiny game cartridges for his hand-held learning device had to be set side by side with all the titles facing upwards. Any sudden movement, act of nature, or accidental bumping of said items that jarred them out of uniformity would prompt swift action. Indecipherable mumbling would serve as the background noise as he returned the disturbed articles back to their rightful position.

Tracy-Ann noticed this behavior one too many times to not be bothered.

"That is not normal," she shared with me.

I may have thought something was out of the ordinary with Trey's behavior, but I wasn't about to criticize him for being neat. I was still finding excuses. "He just likes to keep his stuff in order," I returned. "I wish I was that neat at his age."

I was not ready to believe that every little thing Trey did different meant he had a problem.

At the beginning of 2012 we changed our living environment completely from renting a floor of a home in Brooklyn to owning an entire house in Queens. Trey's behavior began to change over the course of the next few months. He began to act out. There were angry outbursts seemingly out of nowhere. He was still not putting multiple words together so I could not understand him.

Trey would cry at random moments during school nights, hours after he had arrived home. He was still not speaking in depth about how his day in school progressed, so we were left to wonder about the cause of these meltdowns.

Was the change in environment finally affecting him? I was still commuting him to the school in Brooklyn. Maybe the thought of driving to Queens made him feel like he was leaving his home behind. I tried to speak to him, but he could not respond.

Was someone bothering him at school? When we posed this question to Trey it did not illicit a response. It became frustrating not being able to get a clear understanding of the cause of his distress, especially when his teacher was just as vague in her answers.

Could Trey be jealous? At this point Tracy-Ann was expecting our second child. He was about to be a big brother. Before then he had been the sole recipient of all the family's affection and adulation. The primary beneficiary of all toys, gifts, and other spoils of being a one of one.

Maybe he did not want to share anything or anyone he felt rightfully belonged to him. Children are naturally territorial, selfish even, especially when they have been the center of attention. They must be taught to accept change, to share. They must know that they will not be treated differently. It is a lesson that is tough to adhere to in adults let alone a little boy.

JUNE 2012.

The final straw at his school came a few days after Tracy-Ann had given birth to our daughter. I was an unseasonably cool morning, so I dressed Trey according to the weather. The school had a uniform, so he had on an undershirt, the white buttoned-down shirt, navy blue uniform pants, the school sweater, and his jacket. I dropped him off without an issue. When I would pick him up in afternoon I usually walk into the doorway of the class and do a quick scan of the classroom to see how the kids were interacting with each other.

On this day I noticed Trey was not at his regular table. I did not immediately locate him. The room was unusually hot for a summer day. It felt like the heat was on. I looked to the corner left of the room and saw Ms. Kane behind her desk talking to another student. I looked back towards the area by the window and saw a child with his head down on the desk. As I moved closer, I realized it was Trey. I thought this was strange because nap time had ended hours earlier. I attempted to wake him by tapping on his left shoulder, but he did not move. I put my hand on his shoulder and gently moved him while calling his name. He still did not move. Either he was in a deep sleep, or something was wrong. I began to shake him until he finally lifted his head, but he could barely open his eyes. Trey still had on his school sweater. I believed sitting in a hot classroom with all those layers he was overcome by the heat and passed out.

I immediately looked over at Ms. Kane. How did she not notice Trey? I figured she moved his seat because of the complaints of the other child, but her lack of awareness made me furious. When I approached her about this her response was that she thought he was fine because if he was too hot, he would have removed his sweater. It did not make sense to me. Trey possibly suffered from heat exhaustion and this lady was none the wiser.

Though I was angry at her lack of empathy for what happened to Trey in her class, one thing Ms. Kane said that stuck with me was 'if he was hot, he could have taken off his sweater'. As tone deaf and callous as she sounded in that moment it made me think why would he sit there so uncomfortable and not do anything to help himself? Why didn't he say anything to the teacher?

I thought about the boy that complained about Trey 'laughing' at him. He was able to communicate his thoughts to the teacher enough that Trey was removed from the table. In this instance Trey was obviously unable to get the attention of Ms. Kane or figure out a way to cool himself down.

I would be lying if I said I was not concerned about Trey being unable to speak to me. He was five years old. He was clearly frustrated. The look in his eyes spoke to me. I saw a boy who knew what he wanted to say, but just couldn't find the words to communicate it. I could not imagine being unable to speak when I wanted to. Therefore, I did not know how to begin to assist him. My theory of placing him around other kids was not working. I needed help, but I still could not admit it to anyone else.

I had no time to ponder this as I immediately rushed him to the hospital where Tracy-Ann was. The plan was to bring him there after school to see his little sister for the first time. This medical emergency was an unexpected wrinkle. When we arrived at the hospital Trey was put on a gurney and given fluid intravenously. I had alerted both of his Nanas (grandmothers) that he was at the hospital in his own room. When they arrived to sit with him, I went to my wife's room.

Tracy-Ann was sitting up in her bed and to her left Aja was swaddled in her blanket fast asleep. When she asked for Trey, I told her he was in another room in the hospital. I shared with her that he was passed out when I arrived to pick him up from school. Despite informing her that he was alert and receiving fluids, she went into a panic. She got so worked up that she began bleeding. A medical emergency had to be called for her. It was a tense moment as I did not know if she was hemorrhaging.

I immediately regretted telling her about what happened to Trey. I took heat from other family in the room. There was no way I could know my wife would have this reaction.

The nurse came in to look at Tracy-Ann. All she was concerned about was Trey. I left the room to check on him. When I arrived at Trey's room, he had a lot more energy. Being rehydrated, his strength had returned. I asked him if he was ready to see his sister and he nodded.

I made it a point to have Trey walk into his mother's room under his own power to show her he was feeling better. She, in contrast, looked drained. She slowly turned her head and smiled at him as he stood by her bedside. When Trey was finally able to see Aja, he did not show any outward emotion. There were no fits of anger that would lead us to believe he was upset about sharing his parents. On the contrary, he smiled at his baby sister as she lay in his mother's arms in the hospital. Family members showered him with "awws" and other sounds of affection at the love fest they were witnessing.

THE REVELATION

By the time school ended in June, we decided the lack of transparency we were receiving from Trey's teacher was not worth the hassle of driving back and forth. He would look for a new school in the fall closer to home. My wife went on maternity leave to care for Aja. Being home full time allowed her to do a complete unofficial assessment of Trey.

She was able to see all the signs and symptoms up close to validate her belief that Trey needed professional help. She shared her views with me, her mother and sister. I was still not convinced he needed his head examined. I associated that with crazy. I knew my son wasn't out of his mind. He was way too smart; he just wasn't speaking to us. My unwillingness to see her point of view caused major arguments between us. No one was co-signing what she was seeing. I was concerned enough about the consistency of her feelings that I went to my Mom to ask if I exhibited any behaviors when I was younger. She told us what I was saying all along that I was a quiet child. My wife was not convinced.

SEPTEMBER 2012.

Instead of another private school we placed Trey in public school to start kindergarten. Money was still an issue with me as I was making bad financial decisions. At the same time, I was about to embark on a new career in law enforcement.

The new job meant I had to take a massive pay cut. My drop in salary made enrolling Trey in another private school impossible. I was living beyond my means, and I made the choice to keep the overpriced vehicle I purchased, against my wife's wishes, when I had the chance to return it. My ego would not allow me to admit I made a mistake. As a result, the bulk of my paycheck went towards the car and insurance.

Tracy-Ann was still on maternity leave, yet she was paying all the bills. Maxing out her credit cards on groceries and simple household needs. Missed car payments dropped my credit score and my fiscal irresponsibility put a strain on our family.

I was happy we did not have to pay for Trey to go to school. The two private schools were not worth the tuition we spent. I hoped public school would provide a better, more stable educational environment for him.

We met Trey's teacher on the first day. She introduced herself as Ms. Knight. She was a slight, African American woman of medium height. Streaks of gray lined the black hair that fell halfway down her ears. She appeared to be very nice, but all teachers seem this way during what I like to call 'the honeymoon period'.

I believe all institutions have this period where the staff of a school or workplace go above and beyond to make everything look great for about the first week before everything goes back to normal and you realize you have been bamboozled, hoodwinked, led astray.

So, I knew better not to judge Ms. Knight off our initial meeting. I just hoped she would be more transparent in her communication. Besides the new teacher I had to get used to not being able to drop Trey at the door of his classroom. After the 'honeymoon period' parents were not allowed to go into the building with their child.

There was a slight adjustment period for both Trey and us. While there was no separation anxiety there were times when he looked back to see where I was. My natural reaction was to move to help him, but I was immediately stopped by a school safety officer. One of the school administrators assured me that Trey would be directed to his class.

After a few days he seemed to be finding his way. I watched him go up the staircase waving at him every time he looked back until he disappeared from my view. After two weeks he stopped looking back at me altogether. He was a pro now. My boy was growing up.

It seemed like a smooth transition. When I picked Trey up in the evening time it was from the auditorium so there was no real contact with the teacher during the morning drop-off or the afternoon pick-up. That would change soon enough.

Tracy-Ann received an urgent call that brought me to the school early. It was a disturbing claim Ms. Knight made that Trey had attacked her and was sitting under the table. She was very upset, adamant that he had ill intent. When I arrived that afternoon to pick him up, she showed me the bite mark on her arm. It was a visible imprint of multiple teeth marks. I was beyond stunned. We had not known Trey to that point to be aggressive except when I attempted to punish him.

It took me a while to realize the way I was disciplined did not translate to him. It wasn't so much about the changing views of what was acceptable. He knew when he was misbehaving, and his mom called me it was time to remove himself from the area. When he did not listen or acted out, my inclination was to raise my voice to scold him. When I did so, he would get a wild look in his eyes. It was like he was reacting to the sound of my voice. He knew the tone was aggressive and he reacted in kind. I remember grabbing his arms to keep him from approaching me. My anger was causing his aggression. For a child that communicated with his hands I did not want him to use them in a physical manner.

I knew what my fate would be if I ever became aggressive to my mother. I did not understand why that did not translate to Trey. It took me a few months to realize I was setting a bad example. Trey was just mimicking the behavior I was showing him. There was no malice involved, he was just defending himself. It never occurred to me that maybe he did not understand that it was wrong to be aggressive to adults. I did not want to make him feel that it was ok to choose violence. I relied heavily towards verbal correction. Besides, he was taking karate classes at the time. When he started using those moves on me, it made the decision to find alternative ways to reprimand him easier.

I concluded Trey must have been triggered in some way at school. Maybe Ms. Knight yelled at him, and he responded aggressively. She did not divulge what preceded this act of violence and I did not ask. I saw she was angry enough to where I feared she may take drastic action like press charges or sue us. I apologized profusely. Thank God she did not file a complaint.

Ms. Knight did suggest that we have Trey tested. This was huge because none of his previous teachers gave us anything close to this advice. Tracy-Ann was extremely thankful that someone else was saying out loud what she had been thinking for months. She finally received confirmation of what she suspected: Trey needed a psychological evaluation. It was a revelation for me as well. Hearing from this teacher what I had been asking of others but did not really want to know was discouraging. I had no idea where to begin to bring him or what I was testing him for.

We received a call from the school's principal. We were told one of us had to set up an appointment to observe Trey. After the observation, he had to get a neurological and psychological evaluation and submit the results, or he could not return to school.

In the days after the biting incident Ms. Knight started to voice concerns about Trey's behavior. She did not sugarcoat what was happening in her classroom, candor that we desperately needed. We were shocked to learn what was taking place. According to Ms. Knight, Trey would not stay in his seat during school lessons. Instead, he would walk around the room and laugh to himself.

This was a relatively new challenge never divulged by his former teachers. I also noticed Ms. Knight's demeanor was less standoffish. There was no anger or resentment in her tone as she relayed this information to us. It's as if she realized Trey was not a bad child with a behavioral problem. What changed her attitude toward him? It was decided that I would set up a time and day to observe him in the classroom.

On the day of the observation, I dropped Trey at the same place I usually did every morning. This time I was allowed to come inside. He was a little surprised, but happy that I was walking up the stairs with him. Once on the second floor, he made a right turn and I followed, content to let him lead the way.

When we arrived at the classroom the kids were removing their coats. I greeted all of them. I looked over at Trey standing next to me. He seemed comfortable around his classmates so far. Ms. Knight smiled as she told me good morning. She looked at Trey.

"Good morning, Trey."

Trey smiled and waved at Ms. Knight, not looking like a child who despised someone enough to attack them. She also did not look like someone who felt threatened.

"Come children, it's time for circle time."

The kids all came together in a designated area of the class and formed a circle. This was a daily routine where the kids would clap their hands while each child would say his or her name. Trey seemed enthusiastic about this exercise.

"My name is Trey," he said as he smiled and clapped his hands.

Once every child had a turn, it was time to gather around Ms. Knight near the classroom library for story time.

"Ok, Trey. Daddy's gonna go now," Ms. Knight said.

I took my cue to make myself scarce. I was not leaving the building, only the classroom where I would stand outside the door and watch him.

The class library has about five medium-sized wooden shelves filled with children's books. The shelves formed a semi-rectangle around the area which helped to separate from the rest of the room. I looked through the glass square of the door and could see everything. I was also able to hear what Ms. Knight was saying to the kids. As she began to read, I watched Trey rise to his feet and begin walking back and forth in the library area. He wasn't looking at any books just moving around an imaginary path with a smile on his face.

Ms. Knight continued reading to the other children undeterred as if this was no surprise to her. Trey completely tuned out what was happening around him. I continued to watch as she attempted to redirect him back to the group.

"Have a seat Trey," she said as the other kids looked on. Some of them laughed while others looked at him strangely. After a few minutes Trey returned to the group.

"Sit here in front of me," Ms. Knight offered.

Trey sat in front of his teacher with his legs crisscrossed and his hands on his lap. As Ms. Knight began to read again, he started to rock back and forth. I heard a few of the other kids snicker as the movement continued. Trey looked around at the kids who were laughing and smiled at them. It was heartbreaking to watch.

Ms. Knight asked Trey to continue reading the story. He took the book from her and began to read every word aloud without hesitation, something most of the other kids could not do. Once he finished, Ms. Knight led the class in applause. He really liked the attention. He smiled and started rocking back and forth again.

I walked away from the classroom door to look at the artwork posted on the wall. When I found Trey's drawings, I noticed a lot of his art was of a boy drawn as a stick figure with a triangle shape extending from his back. It was a cape. What an imagination.

At lunchtime the kids all left the classroom and walked down two flights of stairs before they arrived at the cafeteria. I had already made my way in and seated myself at a different table out of view. Lunchtime for the kids meant break time for Ms. Knight. There were lunch aides and other teachers scattered around the cafeteria, however none of them were near Ms. Knight's class as other students were entering the lunchroom.

Trey was such a picky eater he would not eat the lunch provided by the school. We packed a lunch of the same foods we knew he would eat with his preferred snacks and a juice box. Each class had to wait to be called to receive their lunch trays. Since Trey already had his food, he was the first to eat, or so I thought. As soon as he opened his lunchbox and the other kids saw the snacks he had, some of the girls slid over next to him.

"I want that," one girl said as she reached for Trey's cookies.

"Give me this," another girl yelled as she grabbed his fruit snacks.

I was in utter disbelief as those kids began taking food right out of his lunchbox. Trey was visibly upset, but he could not find the words to tell them to stop.

I looked around for the teachers, but no one was paying attention. The little girls moved in with such calculated precision that I had to wonder if this was a regular occurrence. I thought about all the evenings when I checked Trey's lunchbox and saw it empty. How he had no problem eating his dinner at night. For a child that was a picky eater he had a ravenous appetite in the evening. I never imagined it was because he was not eating lunch.

With no help in sight from any school staff, I was not about to stand by and watch these little girls take Trey's food, especially when they are about to eat the school lunch. I walked over to the table and reached over Trey's shoulder taking the cookies and fruit snacks away from each girl before they could open it.

"That's not yours," I told the girls in a sing-song voice that masked my building anger.

I put the snacks back in Trey's lunchbox. To say the girls were not happy would be an understatement. In fact, they looked at me like I had three heads.

"You don't belong here," one of the girls snapped at me.

I was so shocked by her response all I could say was:

"Well, I'm here today."

I was so upset at these little thieves. I could not believe the audacity of these little girls. I had to remember they were just children, probably with no home training.

"You have to ask for things nicely, you don't just take it."

I had disrupted their pre-lunch snack at Trey's expense. And for that, I got some of the dirtiest looks ever from a set of kids. This observation opened my eyes in a way they hadn't been before.

While I did not like what I saw, I had to realize kids do what you allow them to get away with. Maybe they started out asking Trey for his snacks and when he did not respond, they started helping themselves.

The next step in the process was a visit to a pediatric neurologist in Brooklyn. His suggestion was to track Trey's brain function. It was kind of surreal seeing wires taped to his head. I had to trust that the endless stream of jagged lines was somehow a normal representation of what was going on in his mind. The doctor said his test showed normal readings.

I knew better. No matter what the machine said I recognized there was something going on. I had wasted enough time making excuses and there was no bigger one than a doctor saying your child is fine.

We thought back to Trey's birth and the fact that he did not cry right away. We wondered if a momentary lack of oxygen may have affected his development. We took him to the hospital for another neurological exam. We believed if we did an MRI on his brain, we could rule out any brain damage. We knew he wasn't going to sit still to go through the machine, so we agreed to have him sedated.

I feared what the MRI would show. We waited maybe less than 45 minutes, but it felt like an eternity. I recalled when they finally wheeled Trey out on a gurney he was still under the effects of the anesthesia. Seeing him laid out like that it really hit home to us that this may be the first of many hospital visits. The doctor walked up to us and told us the MRI was normal. The same answer I got from the private doctor in Brooklyn. What we thought would give us clarity only left us more confused.

Then we tried to wake him up.

"Trey! Trey!" Tracy-Ann called to him.

He did not move. She started to shake him gently to no avail. Naturally she started to panic.

"Why is he not waking up?!" she yelled shaking him aggressively.

The doctor hurried back over to us and advised that the anesthesia would take a few minutes to wear off. At that moment Trey started to move his head to the delight of both of us. His eyes barely open he did not understand why his Mommy was crying. A doctor and a machine had cleared Trey of any brain dysfunction in two separate instances, but we were still not persuaded. It was time for the psychological evaluation.

DR. GARNER

We were nervous from the time we stepped off the small elevator with Trey. As we walked down the narrow hallway, it was a perfect metaphor for our state of mind. It felt like the walls were closing in on our family. This was a potentially life-changing visit for Trey and the fear of the unknown was all-consuming. We were still not on one accord in how we looked at him. Our views of what his behavior meant would be made clearer today.

The psychologist Dr. Faith Garner*, Ph.D., specialized in assessment of children and adults with learning disorders, disabilities, and behavioral issues. She would meet with Trey in her office and put him through a series of tests to gauge his mental and physical ability.

The waiting area was as tight a space as the elevator. There were a few chairs set around a small table with magazines dedicated to different areas of the medical field. There was nothing to keep a child busy while waiting. Luckily, we brought a few of Trey's favorite toys to keep him occupied. He took a seat in one of the chairs and began to play with the small toys. Tracy-Ann and I took a seat on each side of him. The anxiety clearly showed on our faces. 'Nervous wreck' is a term that comes to mind, in stark contrast to Trey who was completely oblivious to the magnitude of the visit.

There was a clear door that separated the waiting area from the back office. Clear glass surrounded the entire space offering a view of different people milling about. A tall, slim woman with glasses and strawberry blond hair tied in a bun appeared from the back and opened the door leading to the waiting area.

We rose to our feet as the woman extended her right hand. We greeted Dr. Garner and she turned her attention to Trey. He looked at her as she spoke to him and nodded his answers to all her questions. We reassured him that it was ok to go with the doctor to her office. He smiled as he followed her, maybe because he was able to take his toys with him.

Waiting for Trey to reemerge was excruciating. We did not know what to think. How I wished to be a fly on the wall in the room with him and Dr. Garner. How did he answer her questions? Was he answering her questions? I had the feeling she was being nice for the sake of Trey but had real concerns that she wanted to share with us. For days I thought about what he did in her office.

After a nerve racking few days, we returned to Dr. Garner's office to hear the results of Trey's evaluation. We hoped it would give us some clarity into what was going on with him. The doctor gave us a manila envelope which contained his assessment. As she spoke, I opened the envelope. Upon reading the first couple of paragraphs, any anxiety we had turned to despair and anger.

Reading the diagnosis from Dr. Garner was a humbling experience. Her observations of Trey's behavior described him as "distractible with periods of spacing out". She wrote that he became "inattentive and repetitive when tasks asked of him became more difficult", that he "had a hard time following direction", and that his speech was "significant for articulation difficulties". His motor planning was described as "poor" and the way he held a pencil as "immature".

Dr. Garner's tests introduced words, phrases, and titles such as *General Language Composite*, *visual abstract reasoning*, *spatial visualization and analysis*, *simultaneous processing*, *visual motor coordination*, and *non-verbal concept formation* into my vocabulary. As I read these words, I had no idea of the meaning. The report stated that Trey was asked to put toy blocks together like the way it was constructed in a picture, and he was unable to do so.

Dr. Garner was convinced he had what was called Mixed Receptive-Expressive Language Disorder (MRELD) with a secondary diagnosis of a commutative disorder. She was basically saying that Trey's issues stemmed from a speech delay.

Tracy-Ann could not wrap her mind around this. It may have been a combination of shock and disbelief, but she refused to accept Dr. Garner's findings as complete. I recall there was a major disagreement with MERLD standing alone as the sole diagnosis.

Tracy-Ann did not believe Trey's only issue was a problem with language and communication. She fought for Dr. Garner to add a rule out to the diagnosis. She dealt with developmentally delayed and medically fragile children daily, yet it took nearly five years to get to this point with her own. In her heart she wanted to believe that Trey would be ok.

Nobody wants to believe their child has a disability and I fought that feeling until the evidence was undeniable. Even worse, I convinced my wife to doubt her training, not to follow her mind, or trust her gut instinct. She knew what needed to be done and she did not act. I knew she was heartbroken, and I was to blame. Sure, she had her family members in her ear telling her she was over-reacting, but I was the one in the home with her with Trey. It did not matter what anyone on the outside thought if we were on one accord. Wishing something isn't true doesn't make it false.

I knew I would have to deal with the emotional repercussions from my wife once the reality set in, but the battle to diagnose Trey took precedence right now. There was a real fear of misdiagnosis, especially where medication was suggested as a preventative method. The thought of Trey being subjected to injections, liquid or pills at any time was an absolute deal breaker. Granted, while medication may work with other children, that was not an avenue we wanted to explore if we could help it.

Dr. Garner became really upset that her findings were being questioned. She was adversarial in her retort, touting her credentials as an expert in her field as if we needed a reminder of who she was. We knew what she specialized in, which is why we came to her in the first place. The attitude rubbed me the wrong way. I never saw a person in the medical field become defiant over a simple suggestion. This was a major bomb being dropped on us. Learning our child has a disability, through the mail at that, was life changing. The coldness of her opposition was completely tone deaf. Tracy-Ann was unfazed and continued to push for the addition to Trey's diagnosis.

She knew that if Trey was only diagnosed with a commutative disorder, he would not receive the complete array of services he needed. She made the case that a child with only a speech delay does not hide under tables, or flap their fingers, or run out of the room when they see rice grains on a television or hear static feedback.

Dr. Garner reluctantly relented and labeled Trey with a secondary diagnosis of Pervasive Developmental Disorder (PDD). PDD refers to a group of five disorders characterized by delays in the development of multiple basic functions including socialization and communication. That did not satisfy Tracy-Ann as she wanted "NOS" added to it. I did not know what NOS meant, but I supported my wife. It was about time I trusted her instinct and followed her lead.

I learned "NOS" meant "Not Otherwise Specified". That characterization meant that Trey was on the Autism spectrum but did not quite meet the criteria to be considered having autism spectrum disorder (ASD).

Wait a minute – did my wife believe our child was autistic? That is a huge difference than having a speech delay. Maybe that is why Dr. Garner was hesitant. Most reputable doctors would not sacrifice their name and license diagnosing someone with a condition they don't believe is present. At the time PDD was a separate subtype of Autism and was not a part of the spectrum which I believe is why she agreed to include it as a secondary diagnosis. Arguing for the addition of the "NOS" did not outright say Trey had Autism, but it left the door open to the possibility.

I was crushed. I had little to no information at that point about Autism, but I associated it with people who never talked. I did not know what the symptoms were for a child who was on the Autism spectrum. It is why children of color are five times more likely to be misdiagnosed or not diagnosed at all. Their behaviors are deemed to be aggressive and the inability to communicate is said to be a language disorder, speech delay, or problems associated with attention deficit disorders. Some physicians are quick to prescribe medication to keep them calm, sending them down an entirely different path of chemical dependency. It was something I never heard discussed in our community, let alone my family.

I thank God for Tracy-Ann standing up the way she did that day.

She let Dr. Garner know in no uncertain terms that she would be seeking a second opinion to which the doctor replied, "that's fine", but in a tone that I could only describe as someone childishly saying, "don't believe me then!" She came across as arrogant at a time when we were vulnerable to the raw emotions of the moment. We were a young Black couple she probably believed had no resources and would get the same result from our so-called second opinion and come crawling back to her. I saw the look in my wife's eye. I knew this was the last time we would see Dr. Garner.

FAITH TEST

Tracy-Ann put on a brave face for her little boy, but in private she was shattered. Trey was babbling as a baby. He was hitting all his verbal milestones from birth to two years old. She began the agonizing process of second guessing all her decision making regarding her first-born dating back to her pregnancy. She did not drink alcohol or smoke. She did not do drugs. She did not take any unnecessary risks. I believed all these things were detrimental to an unborn baby. What could have gone wrong?

My wife revisited her initial pregnancy. A wound she thought she would never have to reopen. She was receiving daily injections of blood thinners for the duration of this pregnancy because it was believed clotting in her blood (remember the bloodwork that went unchecked?) led to her previous loss. Were there side effects from the medication that could have caused an issue?

She was angry at herself for not doing more, for not fighting harder for Trey. She blamed herself for not shouting back at the naysayers (me included), none of whom had a master's degree in social work. She figuratively killed herself for allowing fear to paralyze and divert from what her training had instilled. She too let her emotions cloud her better judgement.

Alone with her thoughts, Tracy-Ann had a lot of time to reflect. She thought about when she first noticed the difference in Trey, around the age of two. He got sick more often than usual with ear infections and flu-like symptoms, but she did not think anything of it. She recalled the series of shots he received and how irritable he was in the days following. Around this time there was an uproar in the media over the possibility of immunizations being the cause of Autism. After speaking to our pediatrician, she reassured us that was not the case.

Looking back, I am very fortunate to still be married. All things considered, the impact of Trey's diagnosis, the lack of attention I gave him during our time at home, and the most egregious act: failing to support my wife when she first expressed her feeling that he had a disability, would have driven most women away. Tracy-Ann shared that she felt real resentment towards me. I couldn't blame her. With the clarity of hindsight, I realized all the warning signs were there: the flapping of his hands when he got excited, the repetition of words, the one-word answers, the inability to color objects within the lines, running away from the television, the lack of eye contact. I looked back at the digestive issues he experienced being unable to keep food in his system, especially dairy products, were all signs I ignored. The time he laughed when he hit his head and split his eyelid open should have set off a ton of red flags.

My hindsight should have been foresight. If I would have taken the time to do any kind of research or follow-up on not only what my wife was trying to tell me, but what I was seeing with my own eyes, Trey would have been able to receive help sooner. What I did not know then was that early intervention services would have helped Trey to communicate, not putting him in a classroom around other kids or in front of a television. I left my son to learn language from cartoons on Nickelodeon Jr. Due to my hesitancy to have him tested we missed the early intervention window, which was from about 1 – 3 years of age. I received a lot of silent treatment from my wife over the next few months as we continued to process what we learned.

I struggled to find the words to explain myself knowing Tracy-Ann wanted to hear nothing I had to say. Truthfully, there was no excuse for my ignorance. I had let her down in more ways than one and all I could hope for is that by doing the work to get Trey the assistance he needed, she would eventually forgive me. I also had to reconcile with myself. All I could think about was if I had listened to her Trey would be further along. I did not know what that meant necessarily, but he would have at least received professional help. I realized my denial was my inaction.

I wasn't taught to interact with kids who exhibited these behaviors. Our interactions when Trey became aggressive were negative, not knowing that he was frustrated. The irony of the situation was that I had written about how important being a father was to me and how I planned to break the cycle of absenteeism that occurred in my life. How I was so happy to have a son to continue my name, build a legacy, and here I was unable to help him when he needed me.

Sure, I was present in the home, but had I been more actively speaking to Trey I would have no choice but to open my eyes to what was going on with him. I could have done more. There was a playground directly around the corner from where we lived. I could have brought him out for some fresh air, put him on the swings or the slide, but I did not. I could have bought a bicycle with training wheels and teach him how to ride, I did not. I was heavy into sports. Did I buy a basketball and help him dribble and shoot, or a baseball and gloves and play catch? I did not.

All those activities required interaction. It required that I speak to him. I was just as negligent as the doctor I condemned.

Luckily, Tracy-Ann was taking him to the park while I was stuck at work. I did not know what would become of Trey or where to begin in terms of treating him. I was genuinely scared that he would never speak. To even begin to help him, I had to get past my personal feelings and learn as much as I could about speech delays, Mixed Receptive Language Disorder, and the Autism spectrum.

I had to get past the stigma I had placed on this community in my own mind. I had a child that was special in a way I never imagined. How would my family and friends view Trey? How would they look at us? Would they treat him like he was disabled? I could not wrap my mind around people I cared about walking on eggshells around us, scared to be themselves because they felt bad for us. I did not want anyone's pity or apology. I had already lost two children and the one I had would not be 'normal'.

I questioned God in that moment. Why us? I looked at my close friends who had children, I looked at my family members who had kids. How would my son carry on my name if he was developmentally delayed? How would he get married and start a family if he couldn't communicate?

There was no way I could tell my family or my close friends. I was too embarrassed. I wrote about how proud I was to be a father to a son, how I was going to raise him to be a great man, give him all the things I never had, teach him all the things I was never taught. How I was going to 'pass the torch'. And now my heir could not even speak to me. He could not speak to anyone. I did not know what I could 'pass on' to him. They would think I was delusional. I was not going to be anyone's charity case. I was effectively going to hide my son's diagnosis.

That's what ignorance does. That's what the devil does. I was not communicating these feelings to my wife at the time. Maybe she would have informed me that my thought process was wrong. She would have told me that people who are autistic can go on to live meaningful lives if they receive the appropriate services in a timely manner. I did not know this at the time. I had no reason to believe Trey would ever speak to me the way I wanted him to. The way that was acceptable to society. After what we experienced with him in the school system to this point, I had no faith. That's a dangerous mindset to have. I was at a crossroads. The way I saw it I had two choices: I could remain in this dark place and give up or I could lift myself up and trust that God will make a way.

I finally started to do some research. Trey needed speech therapy to help with his communication, occupational therapy to assist him with his fine motor skills. We put him on a strict diet of gluten-free products, removing food with dyes and coloring like Yellow No.5, hoping that would help with his hyperactivity.

We met with the administration at his school. During this meeting was the first time I learned of an Individualized Education Plan (IEP). This was a set of educational goals Trey needed to achieve by the end of the school year. We enrolled him in multiple places for speech therapy in Brooklyn and Long Island. We took him to visual therapy believing that he was not being attentive in class because he could not see the board. I was told Trey had a tracking issue, which meant both of his eyes were not moving in the same direction at same time. I could not imagine how that felt, but I was convinced he needed the 30-minute sessions. He was given visual exercises like putting golf tee-looking pegs into holes, reading words, and looking at images with colored shades, and word find worksheets to take home.

NOVEMBER 2013.

We focused on creating more opportunities for Trey to socialize. We noticed his love for soccer, so we did our best to nurture and feed his curiosity by signing him up in a league in Long Island. It was important for us to not only keep him active, but we believed enrolling him in a team sport would allow him to interact with other kids.

When we picked up his uniform it felt surreal. I loved playing organized sports as a kid. There was nothing better than hearing my teammates cheer for me while I was standing in the batter's box or hearing the roar of approval from my coach when I made a good play in the field. To hear my Dad yell 'alright!' when I rolled the perfect ball for a strike, and the high five that met me as I ran back to the top of the lane. He was the reason I loved to bowl. I wanted to be like him.

My Dad never saw me play little league baseball, even though he was the reason I fell in love with the sport in the first place. His passion for the New York Mets was exhilarating and infectious. Still, it was my mother who made my dream of playing baseball in an organized league a reality. It was her boyfriend that was taking me to my games at Marine Park in Brooklyn. I still remember how that made me feel. At the end of my game, win or lose, no excitement or 'you'll get 'em next time' speeches from the new guy in my mother's life. Just a ride back home in a dusty old sky-blue Chevrolet filled with an uncomfortable amount of cigarette smoke that I desperately tried not to inhale. And silence. Deafening silence that sent a message that was loud and clear. He didn't speak to me. He didn't care for me or about me.

This was my son's first foray into organized sports, and I wanted to make sure he saw that I was there for him. The pride I felt when he stepped on the soccer field for the first time in his red jersey with the blue shorts. His black cleats made it official. The red soccer ball we bought for him meshed well with his team jersey.

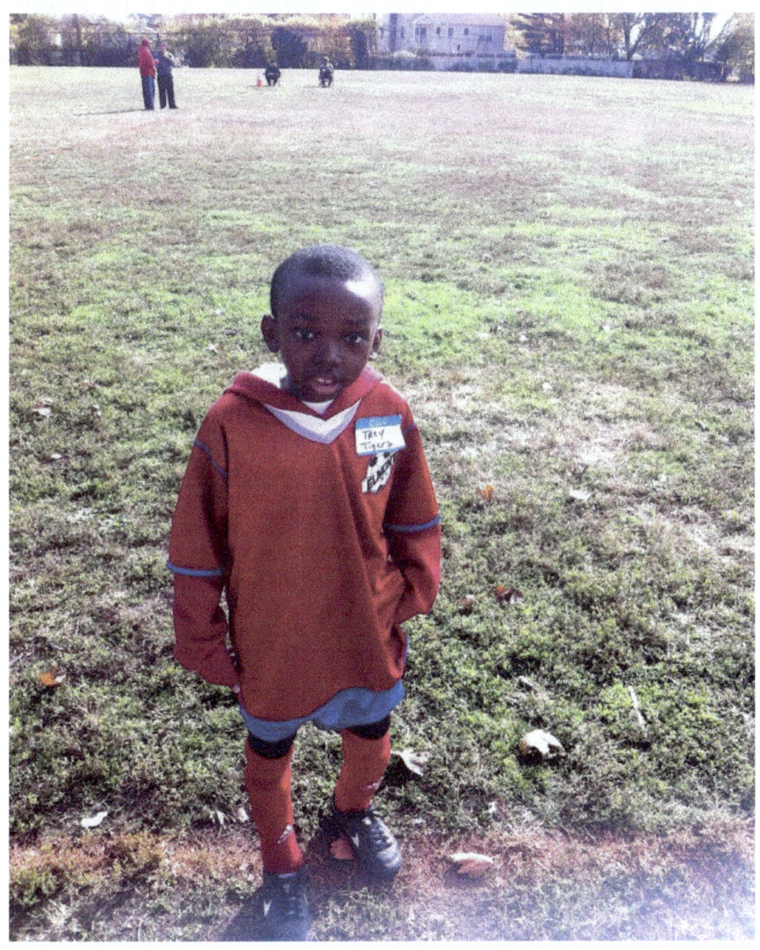

When the coach called his team over to huddle together, Trey would wander off in another direction. The coach would call his name and he would not immediately respond. There were drills that were prepared for each player to demonstrate their skill level. Small orange cones were placed several feet apart. Each player had to maneuver the soccer ball in and out of the cones. One by one we watched each child complete the drill, some struggled, but the main idea of the exercise was achieved.

When it was Trey's turn, he did not immediately start when the coach blew the whistle. He needed prompting from the sideline coach.

"Go ahead, buddy!" I yelled.

"Kick the ball, Trey!"

He finally moved on that command from his mother. Instead of kicking the ball in and out of the cones, which required light pressure on the ball from the sides of both feet, Trey cocked his right leg back and kicked the ball as hard as he could sending it sailing into the air. The coach was stunned. He looked at Trey then at us. We heard the gasps from the parents around us, then murmuring.

"Nice job, Trey!" I yelled out. "Way to kick the ball! Next time, kick it in between the cones."

I saw the look in the coach's eyes as he looked at us then back at

Trey. He was confused.

"Hey Trey," he began. "That was nice, but you have to kick the ball in between the cones." Trey made no eye contact with the coach. He was preoccupied with the ball he just launched. The coach demonstrated what he wanted Trey to do.

"Look here, son."

Coach began to kick the ball lightly between the cones. The movement of the ball finally caught Trey's attention and he followed the movement. Once he cleared three of the cones, the coach kicked the ball back to the starting point. Trey was looking in another direction. I got nervous.

Another exercise required the kids to run sprints. Trey loved to run around so this was right up his alley. The kids were instructed to run towards yellow cones placed off in the distance and run back to the group. Once the whistle blew the other kids took off running.

"Go! Go, Trey!" I yelled.

Naturally he saw everyone else running so he began to run too. Trey didn't run the same way as everyone else, he decided to take a detour. Halfway to the finish Trey started to run to the left.

"No, Trey! Straight ahead!" Tracy-Ann barked.

I heard laughter and snickering. Not from kids, which I would have expected and accepted because children have no interest in sparing feelings, it was some of the adults who found humor in our boy going off track. This was disturbing. They didn't know him. They didn't know if something was wrong with him. How does any grown human being laugh at a child who is lost?

I found that Tracy-Ann and I were doing a lot of redirecting and it quickly became clear that I had to be a second coach on the sidelines. Suddenly a horsefly flew into the space on the field. Once Trey saw it, I knew it was over. Even when it flew away, he looked for it. When it circled around, he swatted at it. From a distance it looked like he was swinging at the air. The game was literally passing him by, but he did not care. The laughter grew louder. My first instinct was to turn to the obnoxious couple and undress them verbally. To poke fun at a child who was clearly trapped in his own world of fear and panic was despicable to me. I wanted to scoop him up and carry him off the field.

I guess I expected more from grown adults. I've seen and heard stories of parents becoming involved in their child's game, arguing bad calls, physically engaging in altercations with other coaches and parents. These were actions I did not agree with and believed have no place in sports. It takes the focus away from the kids. It defies the mantra of good sportsmanship. However, if this was ever the time to get my hands dirty, this would be it. Laughing at a child who for all intents and purposes looks lost goes beyond the parameters of good conduct. It was an eye-opening experience to say the least. I was disappointed in them, embarrassed for Trey, and angry because he had no idea that he was the center of such ignorant behavior.

For a few moments I thought about not bringing Trey back. I felt like I needed to hide him. If adults were going to treat him like this, I can only imagine what kids in school will think of him. The cold reality hit me. Tracy-Ann and I had to put whatever tension we had aside for the good of our son because we were in a bigger battle than we imagined. We just wanted him to meet new friends. Instead, we got confirmation that we needed to be careful bringing him out in public. It was unbelievable, talking about my son like an exotic pet that could not be seen in certain places. It was the fear of being ridiculed, the doubt that he would be accepted for who he is. It was selfish to try to make that decision for him.

I could only imagine what was going on inside of his mind. He was literally living this. I did not know or think to ask how he was feeling about this because I knew he couldn't give me a straight answer. I knew he deserved to be able to enjoy playing sports he loved just like any other child without feeling like an outsider. He deserved to sit in a classroom without the fear of being bullied or laughed at because he did not communicate the way other kids did. He needed a safe environment to play and learn at his own pace with people who were patient, empathetic, and willing to give him the attention to detail he needed. Even though he won a participation trophy, this soccer league was not that place, and public school was not the space.

CATHOLIC SCHOOL

After the fallout from our experience in public school, we tried a different option with Trey. On the advice of one of Tracy-Ann's co-workers, we enrolled him in a Catholic school in Queens for first grade.

Even though we had an official diagnosis that Trey had a developmental delay, we were still not aware of any specialized schools, class ratios, or speech or occupational therapists that we could bring him to on a consistent basis. Hell, I didn't even know there could be more than two teachers in a classroom. When I thought of Catholic school, I equated it with structure, strict guidelines, and stern teachers. I pulled him from visual and speech therapy he was receiving in Brooklyn as the out-of-pocket costs were adding up and I did not see any improvement. We were hoping that this school would offer Trey what he needed.

When we sat down with the principal of the school to meet Trey, all I can remember is this elderly lady trying to get his attention and him being completely distracted by the figurines on her desk. No matter how many times she tried to redirect his attention he would not focus on her for more than a few seconds. He barely responded to his name. I know now that not responding to your name is a red flag for Autism, but that entire meeting should have set off alarms for us. This lady touted how great her special needs program was at the school, yet she could not keep the attention of a six-year-old boy in her office.

It was a heartbreaking visit. I recall getting choked up as I recounted our journey with Trey in multiple schools, just learning of his diagnosis, and hoping they had an answer for us. The principal was comforting and empathetic to our plight, saying all the right things about how there were at least 100 children on the Autism spectrum at the school, and how they are placed based on the requirements of their IEP. She told us Trey would have a speech therapist who would enter the class while it was in session, known as "push-in" service, and assist him. She also told us about "pull-out" service where a therapist would remove him from the classroom to provide individualized services without the distractions of other kids.

It sounded convincing. We were sold on the school, but realistically we did not have any other options. We tried private, public, and now Catholic school hoping to find the right fit for our son. We did not know what to expect. I was still learning all these terms associated with Autism, so we were a prisoner of our own ignorance putting blind faith in people we assumed knew what they were doing.

Like the public school, when dropping Trey off we had to vacate the premises. Kids waited in their respective line in the school yard. It reminded me of my days at Public School 235 in Brooklyn during the first day of school. I was so excited to not only meet my new teacher but see who my classmates would be. Trey seemed to be thrilled about this new chapter in his journey. At the Catholic school kids would arrive and line up in front of their respective teacher until someone blew a whistle to signal it was time to walk into the building. Parents had to clear the school yard once they heard the whistle.

We watched Trey walk into another school building for the first time, but this go-around he did not cry, did not look around for us. There was no separation anxiety. It was my job to pick him up. I would show up at the designated time and wait for the class to appear in the yard. It was at this time where I would formally meet his teacher. There were two teachers, but I knew the lady at the front of the line was the main person. The other lady was the paraprofessional. There were a lot of kids in the class, too many for one teacher to handle.

One day I made the "mistake" of speaking to the paraprofessional. It was only because the main teacher was so busy talking with other parents, I did not see anything wrong with asking my question to the para. The next day it was made clear to me not to approach the assistant teacher at all. In fact, the tone of the teacher made it seem like calling the other lady an assistant was a promotion. It was made to seem like the lady was hired help and had no authority to speak on anything pertaining to the class. It was very weird. I thought to myself 'Why was she there?'

I also noticed that the teacher's mood began to change as the months went by. It recalled the infamous "honeymoon period" I addressed earlier. It hit different now that I knew Trey was on the spectrum. I almost expected an issue at this point. Once the complaints started, mild at first, about him not paying attention and clashing with the other kids, I decided to visit the school.

Like the public school, I would be observing Trey's behavior in the class. Once I arrived, I remember being directed to the classroom and standing outside of the door. The heavy, wooden door was a far cry from the one with the plexiglass at the public school. I had to get the teacher's attention so she would open the door. Once the door was open, I would stand to the side and look inside the room. Trey was seated towards the rear of the classroom on the window side, the furthest away from where I was. I had arrived at the time he was receiving his push-in service from one of the therapists.

One of the things that struck me was the size of the class. I counted over 30 desks and every seat in the room was filled. It was kind of weird trying to watch what Trey was doing and smile at the other kids who were watching me instead of the teacher at the front of the room. She was clearly getting annoyed at my distraction, and it was obvious I would not get a clear picture of how Trey was "disrupting" the class at this particular time.

When I would pick Trey up in the afternoon, I would be one of the first to arrive when they come out of the building into the school yard. The teacher would see me coming from a distance and call his name so he would know he was dismissed. When she stopped greeting me after school let out, I knew something was wrong. Usually, the kids would be in the school yard with the teacher and the paraprofessional to ensure a safe pickup.

Trey's teacher used to greet me with a smile and give me a few words about how he did in class. I knew something was wrong when she would tell him to go to me as soon as I took a few steps into the yard. If he ran to me, I wouldn't have to speak to her. It got to a point where she started turning her back when she saw me coming. She had to look out for the other parents, so it wasn't a coincidence that she suddenly began to look the other way. At first, I did not take offense to the slight, but then as it became more blatant, I wanted to know what was happening in the classroom to make her react in this way. Ironically, I would return to the paraprofessional for answers. The main teacher could not ban me from speaking to the assistant if she was avoiding me altogether.

The assistant would let me know that Trey was doing okay in class but could not offer any clarity as to the main teacher's attitude. There were days when I felt like the main teacher was doing me a favor giving me the cold shoulder because I didn't feel like talking to her anyway, but I knew that stance was irresponsible.

This lady was hiding something. I wasn't going to let it slide like his pre-K teacher.

I received a phone call during the day from the teacher alerting me that Trey threatened to 'kill' another student. I immediately dropped what I was doing and went to the school. Trey didn't have an angry bone in his body. He could barely put sentences together. It had to be a mistake. When I got to the school the teacher looked very distressed.

We did not use that kind of language in the house, but if Trey did threaten a student, they are trained to follow a protocol. I understood that and then I didn't. I believe in a pattern of behavior. She knows his diagnosis. She knew he was the only child receiving pull-out and push-in services. He had no history of disruptive behavior or making threats. Thankfully she called me and not the police.

I couldn't get over this teacher believing that Trey was seriously threatening another student's life. I don't remember seeing the so-called victim of this threat. I revisited the only time Trey became violent in school. Ms. Knight had proof where this teacher was unwilling to divulge specific details. There was a point where I did not believe it happened at all. My mind was spinning with thoughts, many non-flattering. As an educator you are supposed to be the level head in the room. Knowing Trey has special needs did she really think he could kill someone? Or was she trying to get rid of the "problematic" student in an overcrowded classroom?

In this case, it was the word of a woman who was fed up with watching a child with special needs and that was it. I was done with this teacher. Sad part it was too late to remove him from another school. We had to ride out the remaining few months. To compound matters, Trey was not making strides in his communication. When I inquired about his progress with the person tasked with pulling him out of class for speech services, she could not give me a definitive answer. She could not provide any examples of work she did with him. In a fit of aggravation, she blurted out that if she had to gauge his growth from January to June, she would give him the same grade. I remember responding to her that if he has not grown in his communication after six months, she was not doing her job. We learned that she was not consistently pulling Trey out of class for therapy, if at all.

It was a nightmare. Another wasted school year. We felt bamboozled. All the promises and assurances made by the principal at the beginning of the year felt disingenuous, lip service to get our money. We certainly did not receive what we paid for. I remember being so discouraged. Wondering if we would ever find a school for Trey was a real concern at this point.

THE TURNAROUND

Tracy-Ann and I were a bundle of nerves as we walked into a non-descript two-story building in Queens. We were about to partake in the most challenging part of our journey: the fight for Trey's scholastic future. We were set to meet with the Committee on Special Education (CSE)… by ourselves.

This was important because after years of moving Trey from one school to another we had finally felt like we found the right setting for him. It was Tracy-Ann who called me sobbing from the Glen Cove area of Long Island, New York. She was taking a tour of an elementary school named School for Language and Communication Development (SLCD). The title alone spelled out exactly what Trey needed, but I was skeptical about yet another school claiming they could provide the right services for our son. From the sound of my wife's voice SLCD might be the real deal.

Tracy-Ann knows what to look for. Her expertise in social service affords her the insight to locate any red flags. Through a quivering tone she relayed to me the sense of calm she felt as she walked through the classrooms and learned about the curriculum, how it would be implemented in accordance with Trey's IEP, and the temperament of the principal, teachers, and therapists she met. While we went through the song and dance at past school orientations only to be disappointed, this felt different.

I certainly hoped it would be. If he is accepted, this was going to be the fifth school for Trey in a span of five years. He was only seven years old. It was hard for us to enroll him every year in a different school, but there was an issue at every turn. The instability was driving us crazy; I could only imagine how our boy was feeling.

Acceptance was the operative word. The school could welcome Trey with open arms, but since it was a private institution there was a matter of who was going to pay the tuition. Therefore, we were at the meeting with the CSE. We had to convince them to pay for Trey to attend SLCD. The school was recommended by a friend of Tracy-Ann's sister who happened to be a lawyer. The lawyer also recommended that we have legal representation in tow when we go to visit the CSE. They were supposedly notorious for denying funding for private institutions because they believed public schools could afford the same services for children with disabilities. It was our job to prove that SLCD would be a better fit for Trey than public school.

That went without saying for us, we already experienced the challenges of public school with Trey. I failed to see any resources that were conducive to his needs. We had to show the committee that this was not just our biased opinion. We showed up for our meeting as a mother and father deeply in love with our son, willing to fight for his educational life with nerves in the pit of our stomachs, a desperation in our spirit, and the only representation that was in our budget: God.

As we entered the waiting area on the second floor, a wooden desk was positioned to our left and a single row of chairs joined together along the wall directly in front of us. There was no one at the desk so Tracy-Ann and I walked over to the row of chairs and sat down.

Looking around the room there was a small bookshelf filled with books for children to the left, old generic toys were strewn about in a makeshift play area, and the letters of the alphabet were represented by a corresponding picture along the wall above it. Unlike Dr. Garner's office, this space was designed to keep a child occupied.

"Good morning".

We both looked to our right. A petite woman greeted us with a smile.

"Good morning," Tracy-Ann answered. "We have an appointment with the Committee on Special Education."

After we gave our names, the woman disappeared to the back office. The time was growing near and in a matter of moments we would have our child's educational future decided based on how we communicated his needs to people who have never met him.

There was something unique in not having legal representation at the meeting, besides the fact that it was rarely done. It would be guaranteed that two parents would be speaking from the heart, not being spoken for, or hiding behind legal jargon. We hoped the committee would see the humanity in our plight and empathize with what we endured to get to this point.

As we waited to be called into the conference room, the silence was deafening. It seemed like the longer we waited the more the nerves seemingly gnawed at our insides. Suddenly I closed my eyes and grabbed Tracy-Ann's left hand with my right hand.

"Dear God, we thank you for waking us up this morning and allowing us to see another day. We thank you for giving us the opportunity to be here today in this office and meeting with the committee about Trey.

We ask that you guide us as we sit across from the members of the committee, touch their hearts, Father God, allow them to have an open mind and listen to our story. We know that whatever happens it is Your will. In Jesus name we pray, Amen."

I don't know where it came from, but I felt in that moment we needed a reminder of Who was representing us. It was an act of faith specific in its purpose to provide divine assistance to our cause. At that moment the woman returned, and we were escorted to the back office.

SEPTEMBER 2014

The first day at the SLCD Elementary for Trey was the first time I stepped into the school. He did not seem uneasy at all. The entrance looked like the Catholic school, so maybe he believed he was in the same place. Or maybe he knew he had found a home. I was more nervous than he was.

We met the principal Mrs. Katzman, and she was just as nice as every other administrator in the past schools. This time, however, we were not fed any statistics about how many kids with IEP's were in the school. We were just given a tour.

During the simple walk through the hallway, I saw portraits of the founder of the school, the board of directors, children who graduated, and honorary plaques in honor of people who have donated money and resources to the school. What struck me was that every person that walked by us greeted us with a smile or 'good morning'. That may seem like a small gesture, but how staff responds to strangers in their building tells me a lot about how they will treat your children when you leave. I was taking inventory.

When we arrived at Trey's class, we were introduced to Ms. Carucci. Upon seeing us she made a beeline to the door. Her smile was a mile wide, and her attitude was infectious. I had never seen this energy during any 'honeymoon period' before. I was pleasantly surprised to see she was not the only teacher in the room. There were three other adults. They were not parents waiting around, they were paraprofessionals. Four teachers in the room…at once? It was a foreign concept to me.

I counted 12 children in the room including Trey. There were no other children coming in. He was going to receive the individualized attention we had only heard about in the other school. I was cautiously optimistic, but I understood why Tracy-Ann was moved to tears. I met the people who would be Trey's speech and occupational therapist that day.

Even though this would be another transition for us in terms of travel (Trey would now be taking a bus to school for the first time), I prayed that this would be his last educational stop. If we had to send him to Long Island to receive the services he needs, it was well worth it. It was at the Developmental and Behavioral Pediatrics office of Cohen's Children Center in Long Island where we sought our second opinion in the spring of 2014. Trey was officially diagnosed with Autism. He was seven years old.

The impact of the SLCD was immediate. Within a few weeks Trey was speaking to us. In a few months he was able to tell us how his day was. Within the year he was having a full-blown conversation. He was able to communicate when he was feeling pain in his stomach, something he was unable to do in the past.

I will never forget how excited Trey was on the day he was able to show me that he could tie his shoes. It was a momentous occasion indeed. After tying the laces on two pairs of sneakers, he ran back to his room and brought out a pair of shorts to show that he could tie the string into a bow. This was a milestone worthy of celebration. I made sure to shower him with praise for all the little things he accomplished that we took for granted.

We were finally seeing progress. A fact we shared during the annual IEP meeting with the CSE. They were so impressed by our advocacy that they agreed to cover Trey's tuition. God is so awesome! When man said we would need a lawyer to convince them to fund his education, God said trust in Me. He returned all the out-of-pocket costs for the first year at SLCD. The power of prayer is truly amazing. Faith moves mountains!

Trey continued to improve dramatically in his speech and ability to use his hands that his occupational therapy was phased out of his IEP. He was able to dress himself, discern whether his undershirt was inside out before putting it on. Again, tasks that seem so miniscule in the grand scheme of things but was so vital for his development.

By the time Trey arrived in SLCD Middle School, he was talking a mile a minute. He would tell us a story about his day in school and then walk away. Minutes later he would return and talk about something else that happened. This pattern occurred regularly as he went through the task of processing information. He had to tell us everything that popped into his head. It was like he was overcompensating for all those years he was unable to share his thoughts. I understood his excitement, but it was clear he needed help with social cues. It was not what he was saying, but when he was saying it.

The school, soon to be re-christened as Tiegerman Middle School in honor of the founder Dr. Ellenmorris Tiegerman, was in Woodside, Queens. Trey was leaving the comfort of the Elementary school and we were losing the security of their dedicated staff. This was just as much a transition for us as Trey.

Tracy-Ann and I had to acclimate ourselves to an entirely new group of teachers and administrators. I took solace in the fact that a lot of the kids he had made friends with at the elementary school were coming to the middle school with him.

Middle school meant Trey was getting older. It meant more independence. He would be following a bell schedule and moving to a different classroom for each subject. I recalled that feeling when I was in I.S. 383 in Brooklyn. Walking to hallways in search of my next class gave me a feeling of responsibility. I had a locker to store my books for the first time. It was a great experience.

The comfort of seeing familiar faces helped Trey transition. He let us know who was in his class, he also knew the names of all the teachers. He had a speech therapist and now a counselor to help him socialize in a group setting.

During the first parent-teacher conference we received a relatively good report about Trey, however practically every teacher had the same concern. Trey was tapping on his desk throughout the class. It got so bad that he was distracting the other kids. We addressed it with him hoping that since we knew about it, he would stop. Months later at the second parent-teacher conference the issue came up again.

This time we told Trey that there was a hidden camera in every classroom and that we were able to see when he was not listening to the teacher. We were told that this strategy had worked. I noticed at both conferences the only person who did not have an issue with Trey tapping was the music teacher Mr. Zoly. This young man was a ball of energy when I first met him. He had to be fresh out of college. He described the course of study and showed us the instruments the students were playing. He even showed me a music application that could be downloaded on the mobile phone. The app showed a group of faces each with a distinct expression. When you touch the face, it comes alive with sound. Each face created a different sound of instrument. When multiple faces were touched their sounds combined to make a gorgeous crescendo of music.

I wondered if this was the sounds Trey was hearing when he was tapping on the desk in the other classes. I thought about when he was younger and how he was fixated on the man playing the piano in 'chapel' when he was in prekindergarten. How that inspired him to play the ironing board at home. How he played his toy drum perfectly in tune with the music on the cell phone when he was two. I realized we did not cultivate this gift for playing music that he had.

Trey showed us at a young age what he was interested in, and we totally missed the sign. We enrolled him in piano lessons immediately. This was a new frontier for all of us. Would he be able to sit and listen to instruction? We used an old keyboard we had sitting in the house. This was Trey's first time having a formal lesson playing an instrument. Not only did the teacher want to see what he knew, but I was curious to see as well.

I always wanted to play the drums and guitar as a kid, but I never had the opportunity to learn. I was going to live vicariously through Trey. The lessons took place in our living room. The teacher, an older lady named Ms. Joseph, had to commute to our house. In their first meeting we advised her that Trey was on the Autism spectrum. She was surprisingly undeterred. She worked on hand placement on the keys and learning theory.

After a few lessons I realized Trey was not interested in music theory, he just wanted to play. He had an interesting taste in music. He had a small radio in his room, and it was always tuned to CBS 101.1 FM. That station played a lot of pop and rock music from the 80s. This was music I had grown up listening to. Every time I turned it on in my car, I would see his head in the rearview mirror pop up from the back seat looking to see the name of the song and artist. I later learned, from Trey, that one of his teachers kept a radio in his classroom tuned to this station. It got to a point where he could rattle off the song title and artist of any song that came on. From Bon Jovi, Phil Collins, Cyndi Lauper, to A-Ha, Michael Jackson, and Billy Joel. He was an encyclopedia of classic rock. Go figure.

It wasn't long before Trey began playing these songs on the keyboard. I knew for a fact Ms. Joseph never taught him "Living on a Prayer", yet there he was playing the song. It was extraordinary. At the same time, we learned Tiegerman Middle

School had formed a rock band comprised of students. This was an opportunity for Trey to showcase his skills to his peers.

Trey wanted to play the drums, but another student had already been assigned to it. He was accepted into the rock band on keyboard. Not only was he getting lessons at home, but he was applying what he learned and receiving additional counsel at school. We never heard about him tapping on his desk again.

Being in the rock band offered the opportunity to showcase what Trey learned in the spring concert. Tracy-Ann and I were so excited to see him perform. He took part in plenty of school productions in the elementary school, but that was all singing and dancing with his entire class, never playing an instrument.

JUNE 14, 2019.

We were two of many proud parents who filed into the school cafeteria to see the performance. The backdrop had the theme from the movie School of Rock featuring Jack Black. Trey took his place behind the keyboard. Another young man sat behind the drum set, another picked up the guitar, and a young lady stood behind the microphone stand. The teacher in charge of the rock band, Mr. Formont, had his own bass guitar and sat on a stool next to the drums. At his direction the kids launched into the song

"Teacher's Pet" featured in the film.

I had my camera phone recording the moment beaming with pride, but I was not ready for what was next. When the song ended, I'm leading the applause, clapping, hollering, making sure Trey sees us cheering him on.

Then it happened.

Trey moved from behind the keyboard to center stage. He took his place behind the microphone. The young lady stepped aside but remained to his left. Tracy-Ann and I looked at each other. As the music began to *"It's a Long Way to the Top"* by AC/DC a high-pitched voice began to sing the first verse. There was another young man standing to the right of Trey, but his mouth was not moving. The singing kept going.

In all the concerts in elementary school Trey sang as part of an ensemble. I hadn't heard him sing since he was a toddler belting out those gospel songs in the house. That was cute then, but when I finally realized what I was hearing, I was floored. I looked to my left and saw the tear lines had already made tracks down my wife's cheeks as she struggled to zoom in to Trey on her phone. Our boy was singing lead in the school rock band.

I had to let that sink in. When it was over, I gave him a standing ovation. Ever since Trey started at Tiegerman we celebrated every milestone reached big or small. This was totally unexpected. Everything that he was lacking before, that we were told he would never have: the eye contact, the swag, the confidence, all that we asked God to instill in Trey, he showed us that day. God was telling us to have faith, that He was giving our child back to us. On that day we saw the evidence of what God revealed: that Trey could do anything if we put Him first. I thought about Dr. Garner who was so negative in her assessment, basically telling us Trey would never speak. The private school teachers who knew something was wrong with him, but never said anything directly to us.

Through a speaking engagement at Aja's daycare Mona Prep, I learned that teachers are advised not to directly share their belief that a child may be developmentally delayed and need services. I assumed it was for their own personal safety. If this was true it explained why his teachers prior to Ms. Knight never said anything. As frustrating as Ms. Kane was, this kind of clarified what her thought process was. I remember one of the teachers approaching me after my presentation at Mona Prep begging me to come back and speak because there were so many parents in the room who were in denial about their child. She said she would get into arguments with parents. I did notice a lot of the men in the audience with their head down as I spoke. It is tough to hear that your child may have an issue. Not too long ago I was that man.

If Ms. Kane would have shared what she felt about Trey with me, it would have made a difference. Ms. Knight not only gave her advice, but she also showed me the evidence through observation.

It made a difference. I finally got it through my thick skull that my son needed help and my personal feelings were stifling his growth. I wanted to make sure I sent that message loud and clear to the parents at Mona Prep. In dedicating my life to making amends for my ignorance, it was imperative that I share my story. If one person left that day seeking help to rule out a diagnosis, I succeeded.

A diagnosis of Autism was not the end for Trey. It was just the beginning. I was seeing the evidence. Tiegerman school was doing so much for him. They were truly a godsend. There had to be a way that I could show my gratitude.

THE AMAZINGLY AWESOME AMANI

OCTOBER 31, 2015.

Trey dressed up as Superman for Halloween. A simple costume choice at the time. Less than two years later the outfit would take on a whole new meaning. The idea came to me in the shower, as they often do. A story of a boy who has difficulty speaking in real life but dreams of becoming a superhero that saves others when he falls asleep. It was a storyline I kept repeating in my head until I was able to reach a pen and paper. I would incorporate his entire family: Mommy, Daddy, and a younger sister. It was Aja who would come to us and complain about Trey. She would ask us why he would not talk back when she spoke to him? Why was he laughing at her? Why did he seem so weird? Why do we love him more than her? All valid questions under the circumstances. I realized these were most likely the same inquiries Trey's former classmates had.

As we took the time to explain to Aja that Trey meant no ill will towards her, that he could not help the way he responded to her, she became less angry at him and us. She realized we did not love him more, but that he needed help to be able to communicate with her. As her understanding of what autism spectrum disorder was the more protective she became of him in public. At home, however, she had no interest in being patient. She demanded Trey talk back to her. She talked his head off. He had no choice but to respond. I will tell anybody that Aja is just as responsible as any speech therapist for Trey being able to speak.

I imagined all those instances where Trey was frustrated and acted out at home. When he had those unexplainable temper tantrums. I ventured a guess that he was tired of not being able to speak when he wanted to. It is extremely maddening to know what you want to say in your head, but the words do not come out of your mouth. The point of having him fall asleep is a metaphor of him dreaming of being able to communicate. I was literally giving him a voice.

This became an important part of our journey because I was using my writing background to share important information about a condition that hundreds of thousands of people are dealing with. Instead of talking at people with speeches or boring presentations, we were using literature to promote awareness.

I had to adjust my writing style to appeal to children. I was used to writing long stories, in fact, I was writing this as a chapter book until Tracy-Ann convinced me that a picture book would have a greater impact. The idea was to pull the kids in with the visual of the superhero and laden the story with the messages we were trying to get across to the parents. I did not want to be too direct with the first book, so I made subtle hints about who Amani was. Everything that I observed Trey go through in school I was able to interpolate into the story.

Representation mattered as well. It was not lost on us that there was a lack of children's books with Black boys on the cover. We wanted to make sure kids saw themselves in our book. Most importantly, that Trey saw himself as a hero because he was one to us. I don't think I could have faced the challenges he did and manage to keep a smile on my face through it all.

The Amazingly Awesome Amani debuted on April 4, 2018, just in time for Autism Awareness Month. We were intentional in setting the release date. It was our first foray into children's literature. It was a huge accomplishment worthy of a celebration. We decided to do a book launch at my former job: The Westin. It was a full circle moment. Many of my former co-workers were still working there six years after I left. This would be a triumphant return to the place I called home away from home for seven years.

We pulled out all the stops for this event. We had banners made, a stage set up for an exclusive reading of the book, and a cake in the image of the book cover. We paid for convention services to provide food. We had a step and repeat for pictures and a red carpet. Once I began to see the people stream into the ballroom, it hit me that we were officially children's book authors.

The young man of the hour and the reason we were here, Trey was excited to be the subject of all this admiration. I invited him onstage so we could read the book together. Before the reading, I said a few words about the premise of the book and who it was based on, formally revealing that Trey was autistic. It was the first time my Mom and sister had heard it out of my mouth. My best friend's mother was also in the audience that day. My cousin Sherry, who flew in all the way from California to be there, received the news as well. Everyone who did not attend would learn about his diagnosis through the numerous posts on our social media timelines.

It felt like a heavy burden was lifted that day. I did not realize how freeing it would feel to finally tell our truth, to speak about the secret we kept hidden far too long for fear of ridicule. We knew we could not raise awareness if we were not being honest with the people we were trying to reach.

After the reading, pictures were taken in front of the step and repeat, and I sat down to sign copies of the book. The launch went well. The energy of the event really boosted my confidence. I was ready for the next event.

We went on our grind to bring notoriety to our independent title. Without the power of a major publishing company behind us, we knew we had to do a lot of work on our own to get noticed. One of our biggest sacrifices was getting a vendor booth at the annual literary convention Book Expo/BookCon at The Jacob Javits Center in New York City. Over the course of five days, we were able to meet educators, librarians, writers, publishers, and, most importantly, people who have or know friends who have children on the Autism spectrum. People were immediately drawn to our banner of the Black super boy with the confident pose. When we told them the book was about Autism and it was based on our son, the outpouring of support was more than we could have ever imagined. When Trey came to our booth for BookCon that weekend, people were eager to meet him. It was humbling to know that something we created was having such an impact.

It was our first time on a grand stage at one of the signature literary events of the year and I loved every moment interacting with the public. I felt at home in our booth, a huge step and repeat emblazoned with our book cover towering behind us.

I was amazed at how many people shared their own personal stories of family members who were on the spectrum. I was also pleased to see people buying the book to show a Black superhero to their little ones.

We did not want to be a one-book wonder either. Consistency in our promotion of Autism awareness was key. The last thing we wanted to do was champion this great cause, bring attention to a topic that was not discussed, and then disappear.

We booked reading events at multiple Barnes & Noble bookstores in Long Island, New York City, Brooklyn, and New Jersey. We signed up to be vendors at various festivals such as the Harlem Book Festival, the Schomburg Literary Festival, the Baltimore Book Festival, and the Brooklyn Book Festival to name a few.

SEPTEMBER 2018.

We signed up for the annual Autism Speaks Walk. "Team Amazingly Awesome Amani" showed up at the South Street Seaport in our custom-made t-shirts and walked for the cause. It was exhilarating. Trey knew that we were all there in his honor and he loved every moment of it.

We mingled with other groups representing their respective family members on their T-shirts, but no team came close to the sky-blue shirts with the signature green "A" surrounded by the neon yellow puzzle pieces! In my most humble opinion.

When the announcement was made to start walking, we were amongst a sea of people moving for a cause that was bigger than us all. As we crossed those streets in lower Manhattan, I thought about how a year ago I never thought I would be advocating for Autism acceptance. The size of the crowd showed me this is a condition that affects many people. If I could play a part in sharing information that could lead to someone making the decision to test their child, I'm here for it.

More importantly, our promotional efforts seemed to be working. The word was getting around. People were buying our book. By the time we were ready to release the next book, we had done two reprints.

AWESOME
AMANI
BE A HERO

June 10, 2019
The Amazingly Awesome Amani
TAKES ON JITTERS & FEAR

What I took the most pride in was reading to kids. It was a challenge to not only write in language that would appeal to children, but to read in a voice that would keep them engaged. Reading to Aja's class I was able to hone my chops. I knew I wanted to be as interactive an experience as possible. I looked for places in the book where I could get the kids involved. One of the ways I figured to keep them focused was to allow them to scream.

The kids loved the pictures of Amani playing different sports and drawing pictures in school. He was just like them in that regard. The way I changed my voice to a little boy in distress causing Amani to leap into action. Having him save a boy's ball from a bigger kid allowed me to speak on issues of bullying without being preachy. I wish I was able to read this book to Ms. Knight's class.

APRIL 2019.

Our second book in the series *"The Amazingly Awesome Amani Takes On JITTERS & FEAR"* was released on Autism Awareness Day. We wanted to pay homage to the school we felt saved Trey's life. We set up a book fair fundraiser at the Barnes & Noble in Carle Place to raise money for Tiegerman, did a live reading at the school auditorium, and were even featured on Fox 5 News New York where Trey replied on the broadcast: "I'm just awesome!"

In this book we wanted to address the importance of getting acclimated to new surroundings and the effects it has on the emotions of a child on the spectrum. In real life Trey started his first day at SLCD like a champ, but that is not always the case when there is a change of environment. It was important to note that this was not just an "Autism" book. Anyone can feel jitters or fear when starting a new job, new school, or meeting new people in an unfamiliar setting.

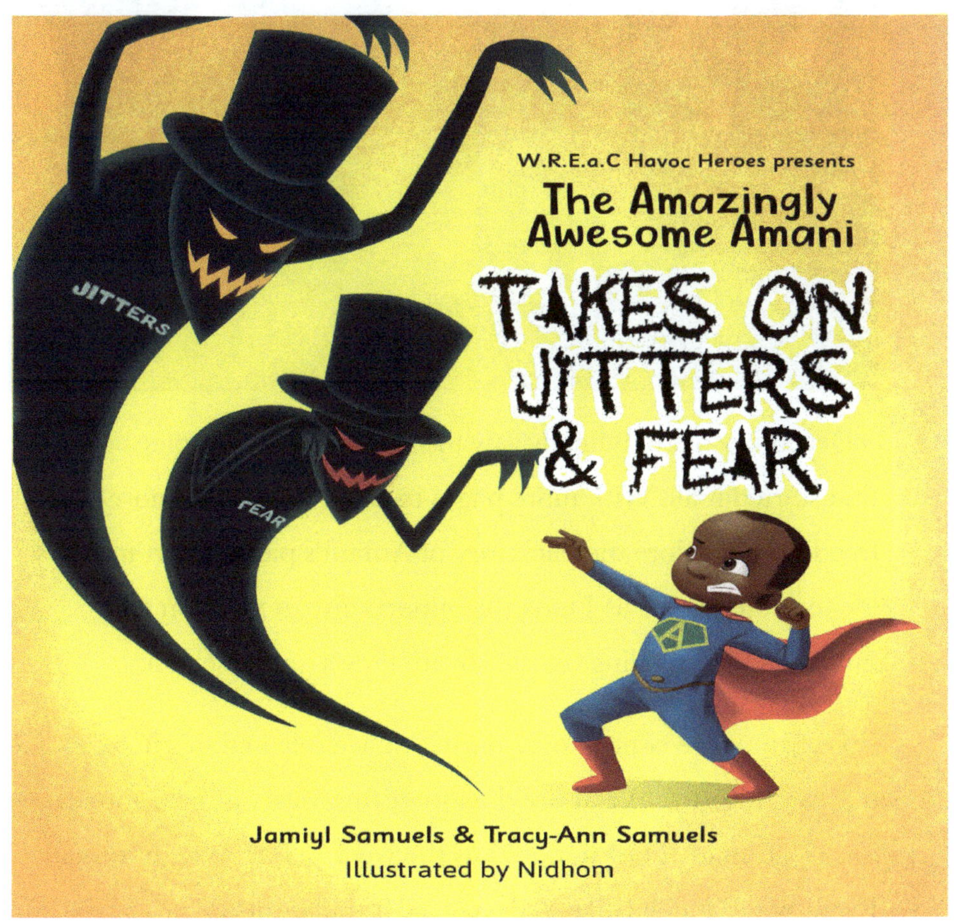

December of 2019 finally saw the release of the chapter book that started it all. With more pages to work with came more freedom to explore the backstory of Amani's parents. Art imitates life to some degree as I took the opportunity to mention the infamous food stealing disaster from Trey's public school.

To gain more control over our work, we released this book under our own imprint. We also did another fundraiser to raise money for Tiegerman. They honored us the week before at their annual Evening of Honor Gala. We received a philanthropy award for our fundraising efforts on their behalf. The highlight of the night for me was Trey. Unbeknownst to us he had already prepared a speech in school. When he stepped to the microphone, I was stunned not only that he was reading the speech so well, but he made eye contact with the audience. He looked around and back down at his speech as he thanked the teachers and therapists that helped him along his journey. I looked over at Tracy-Ann and saw a mother who was filled with joy. With tears streaming down her face, I could only imagine what she was thinking at that moment. I marveled at how he was able to write his thoughts and share it so eloquently. I clearly underestimated how much he had improved.

The message we communicated in our children's books was that kids on the Autism spectrum could do the same things as kids who were not on the spectrum. I realized it wasn't until I saw Trey speak that I finally believed it. He was still amazing me.

THE AMAZING ADVENTURES OF
AWESOME
AMANI
A W.R.E.a.C Havoc Heroes Series Book 1
WRITTEN BY JAMIYL SAMUELS & TRACY-ANN SAMUELS
ILLUSTRATED BY ISRAEL RAMIREZ

The COVID-19 pandemic of 2020 did more than delay the release of our third book *The Sensationally Super Sandy*. The subsequent shutdown meant two kids in proximity of each other all day and every day. The more Trey worked on his speech, the more he learned how to find the words to defend himself. Hearing our two kids argue and fight, and tattle on each other was equal parts annoying and refreshing. Aja was once again the unwitting barometer on which we used to gauge Trey's communicative progress.

There were times when he would come to us and complain about his little sister, then there were other times when he would take matters into his own hands. We knew when the latter happened because Aja would emerge from his room in tears. No matter how many times we told her to leave her brother alone, she continued to underestimate him based on her successful attempts to manipulate and coerce him to do her bidding.

One thing we learned was that Trey had a mind of his own – when he felt like it. There is nothing like a little sister who doesn't get what she wants to stir up trouble. This led to a lot of 'he said she said' versions of stories whenever we got involved. The one thing we could count on: whatever Trey's version of the story was most likely the truth. He was incapable of lying. He did not know how to be verbally deceptive. Let Aja tell it, he was extremely adept at bending the truth. This back-and-forth dynamic led to an epic sibling rivalry that would raise any parent's blood pressure.

It was a story I explored when it came time to write Aja's book. The protagonist, based on one of Aja's middle names takes issue with her brother because he does not communicate with her and seemingly smiles and laughs at her expense. Drawing from real conversations we had with her, we were able to identify Autism as the reason behind Amani's behavior.

Relaying the information to Sandy and watching her growth from someone who was insensitive to empathetic was symbolic of how we wanted readers – kids and adults alike – to respond. Having Sandy be able to apply what she learned in real time at her school was such a full circle moment. It just puts a bow on the initial trilogy perfectly. You know the feeling when you are writing, and you don't realize that you are setting certain things in motion until you sit back and look at the completed version? It's amazing how things fall into place so seamlessly.

NEW LIFE

APRIL 28, 2019

A Sunday morning that began normal enough. We were scheduled to travel to New Jersey in the afternoon as invited guests to the launch party for a new company that sold bundles of children's books with Black faces. We were there to read our book "*The Amazingly Awesome Amani*" to the kids and adults in attendance. I was resigned to spending the morning in the house in preparation when Tracy-Ann approached me and said we were going to New Life Pentecostal Church.

New Life is a church also located in New Jersey. Tracy-Ann's co-worker had been pleading with her for years to visit the church. It had been two years prior that we ran into her at Dorney Park. It was their annual church trip. We just so happened to be there as part of a bus trip with our own place of worship. Her co-worker was adamant that she visits the church. Our issue was the distance. "New Jersey was so far from Queens" we reasoned. Was it worth being stuck in traffic for a couple of hours? We even met the Pastor unbeknownst to us. Tracy-Ann was able to spot the Bishop out of thousands of people in the park. That was definitely a sign from

God, and we completely missed it making excuses. It's a funny thing about excuses: it's convenient, it gives us justification for being disobedient.

On this particular morning, I did not hesitate to agree with going to this church before our event. We were in the area, and I believed a little blessing would not hurt. I did not go with the intention of making this my permanent house of worship. I mean, who was going to drive to another state every week for three hours of service? From the moment we walked into the sanctuary, the place was on fire. The Bishop Karel Gray was on the stage, and he was praying for the congregation.

I was immediately struck by his confidence, the forcefulness and command of his voice as he moved from one side of the room to the other. It was a prayer of deliverance. Bishop Gray prayed for Tracy-Ann and me that day. It was like he saw all the pain and baggage we carried into the sanctuary. I realized it was not an accident that we stepped into church at that time almost two years after our initial meeting in the amusement park. God always brings you where He needs you to be. After that initial visit we decided New Life Pentecostal Ministries would be our new spiritual home.

I could speak forever about how the church changed my life, but most importantly I gained wisdom. I gained support from the brothers in the church. I had never seen so many men unapologetically crying out to God, unafraid to share their emotions in a public setting. In Bishop Gray I gained insight into what a true leader looks like. Not only regarding how he directed the church, but as a husband and father in his home.

When we had a reading and book signing event for *"The Amazingly Awesome Amani"* at Barnes & Noble in Holmdel, New Jersey the Bishop's family and other members were there to support us. The way the entire congregation at New Life embraced us was beyond inspiring. Allowing us to share our journey with Trey and taking the time to pray for him.

I told Bishop Gray that Trey plays instruments and without a second thought he suggested Trey join the Praise & Worship music team on the guitar. Without hearing him play, Bishop chose to include him in one of the most vital parts of the ministry. He showed faith in Trey that day, no judgement, or preconceived notions, unmoved by his knowledge of Trey's diagnosis. The most important part of our journey has been getting Trey to socialize with others. We advocate for inclusion for the special needs community and to see Trey be able to utilize his musical talents to 'play for God' every Sunday is inspirational.

You cannot underestimate the power of prayer in the entire equation. We have given our son to the Lord, first when he was baptized, and numerous times through prayer from Pastors of other places of worship over the years. This time felt different. He had a role in the ministry, and it was a responsibility he did not take lightly.

This prayer from the book "Prayers That Avail Much" by Germaine Copeland stood out to me particularly: it encapsulates every emotion that I was feeling:

Father, in the name of Jesus, I thank You for this very special child. You see my confusion, anxiety, frustration, and bewilderment as I attempt to rear him [tenderly] in the training and discipline and the counsel and admonition of the Lord. Forgive me for times when I knowingly or unknowingly irritate and provoke him to anger [exasperate him to resentment].

You see my intense pain when I observe the rejection this child suffers by adults who speak harsh words against him and our family. Children refuse to play with him, and it hurts even though I understand. I know that those who have never walked in our shoes cannot fully understand us.

But, Lord, where others are unmerciful and unkind, You are merciful and kind. Surely, goodness and mercy shall follow us all the days of our lives, and we shall dwell in Your house forever. Hide us in the secret place of Your presence and keep us secretly in Your pavilion from the strife of tongues.

Lord, perfect the fruit of my lips that I may offer to You effective praise and thanksgiving for this child who is a blessing from You.

PANDEMIC

The COVID shutdown allowed us to really focus on Trey's progress. He was a year away from graduating middle school and we wanted to make sure he would be ready for high school level work.

The advent of remote learning was a blessing in that we were given insight into how Trey was learning during the day. What we discovered was that he was not being held accountable for his mistakes on homework questions and exams. This was a major red flag because Trey always trusted what the teachers told him, as he should. So, when we tried to tell him he was wrong, he became confrontational in his defense.

His logic when it came to his schoolwork was that if the teacher did not mark him wrong, his answer was correct. This was troubling to say the least. We did not believe in social promotion, and we made sure we addressed our concerns with the teachers.

The last thing we wanted to see was staff believing because Trey was autistic, he was never going to learn the work. In fact, the opposite was true. It was our experience that if we explained to Trey how to solve a problem, he was able to catch on and do the work. We became more hands-on with his classwork, communicating with teachers on Zoom during his class and via email.

Perhaps because they knew we were closely monitoring Trey's work, we started to receive detailed updates and study guides from teachers that weren't as transparent. Holding the people in charge of educating your child is an important part of advocacy. We also had to make sure Trey was doing his part. We allowed him to do his homework on his own to foster a feeling of independence. We soon learned another challenge was getting him to consistently focus and apply himself.

One of Trey's biggest issues since before he was diagnosed was reading comprehension. While he was able to read the words on the page at a prolific clip, he could not summarize what he read. For the life of me I could not understand how he would get multiple choice questions incorrect. When I found out he was just circling random answers I had a fit.

Did he not understand what the question was asking? No. He chose not to look back at the story to find the answer. How did I know this to be true? I would ask him to read the story in front of me and then look at the questions. He would always choose the right answer when pushed to do the work. He had a bad habit of not trying. We would always drive home the importance of studying.

2 Timothy chapter 2 verse 15 is Tracy-Ann's favorite scripture to use as a reminder: *"Study to shew thyself approved..."* she would say. I know Trey and Aja get tired of hearing it.

Trey was what we called 'wrong and strong'. He had to get his point across at all costs, mostly at the expense of active listening. While it gets really frustrating at times, we realize that he is still a work in progress in that regard. It is easy to forget that we prayed for him to be able to communicate in this way not too long ago. For him to be able to speak what is on his mind is huge. It is easy to take for granted how far he has come.

When the world shut down in March 2020 due to the coronavirus outbreak, we as a household decided to start a daily prayer line. Every morning at 5 o'clock in the morning our phones would ring, and we would sing songs of worship, read a scripture from the Bible, and each person on the line would pray. Guess who would lead us in each area.

When Trey was diagnosed on the spectrum never did I imagine he would be leading our prayer line in gospel songs, choosing and reading scriptures that was placed in his spirit. We prayed to God so many days and nights during this journey and to know that the Lord is speaking through Trey every morning is a blessing.

APRIL 7, 2020.

The death of grandma had a huge effect on everyone. She took her last breath at 6:45 am while Trey and Aja were asleep. Due to concerns over the outbreak of COVID-19 less than a month earlier, they were keeping their distance in their room.

The night before when her primary doctor confirmed that she was transitioning, we allowed the kids to speak to grandma over the phone. While Aja cried every day and shared her anger at not being able to say goodbye to her in person, Trey did not share his grief until over a month later at the in-home birthday party we threw for Tracy-Ann.

After dinner was complete, we noticed he was sitting at the edge of the sofa looking down at the ground. We assumed he wasn't feeling well. He shared that he was sad because he was expecting grandma to join the celebration. We all process grief differently, but this being his first experience with death, we had to pay close attention. Grandma often said she loved Trey as much as Tracy-Ann. If you knew her, that was an unexplainable amount of affection. It was clear he felt her love. We encouraged him to share what he was feeling, and he continued to repeat "I thought grandma would be here." Shortly thereafter he disappeared to the bathroom.

A similar reaction occurred during our Thanksgiving dinner. This presented a different challenge for us of dealing with the loss of a family member. After weeks and months of comforting his mother and sister when they would breakdown emotionally, we finally saw his response to grandma's death was that he became physically ill.

Part of the healing process included moving him into grandma's room, after we removed all her furniture and repainted the room of course. I am sure she would not have wanted it any other way.

LEGACY

As far back as the beginning of creation having a son to carry on the legacy was important. In the Bible, God was specific about family lineage beginning with Adam, to Noah, to Abraham, Isaac, and Jacob, having an heir was paramount. Men are supposed to be the spiritual leaders, the head of the household.

When Trey turned 11 over four years ago, I thought I achieved a great accomplishment. I congratulated myself, even my wife Tracy-Ann mentioned it. My father left my mom and I for good during the summer before my 11th birthday, so I believed I had succeeded in breaking the cycle of abandonment simply by remaining with my wife and my child longer than he did.

When I self-published my book "*Pass The Torch: How A Young Black Father Challenges the 'Deadbeat Dad' Stereotype*" over ten years ago, I celebrated fathers who chose to stay in the lives of their children, myself included. It was cathartic for me as the book was the first time that I communicated how I truly felt about my Dad leaving. However, as I stated in the book, I never got the opportunity to have the conversation with him about what happened. I never heard his side of the story. Did I really heal? Yes, I was present in my child's life, but was I doing enough for him as a father?

In the ten years I shared with my Dad, I learned how to bowl because he was in an organized bowling league and I wanted to do the same. We kicked a soccer ball around in Prospect Park in Brooklyn on certain evenings. I fell in love with baseball because he introduced me to the sport at the same park by playing catch with me and watching Mets games at home. Although it was my Mom who paid for me to play Little League Baseball a little over a year after my father's departure, the seed was already sown.

Trey played briefly in a soccer league, played one game of organized Little League baseball, and a few games in a father/son bowling league with me. Signing him up for baseball was a last-minute decision and a practice with his new team exposed that he did not know the fundamentals of the game. Whose fault was that? His soccer experience ended when he ran off the field at the sight of a dragonfly. I never took him to the park and kicked a soccer ball, let alone taught him how to block out distractions. While we finished the bowling season, my work schedule put an end to any future play in a league.

I was also devastated by Trey's Autism diagnosis. More than I ever wanted to admit. This felt like a double whammy, a shot to my dreams of "passing the torch" to my progeny. We were so focused on getting him services so he could speak properly, then it was an issue of him being able to function around other kids who were not on the spectrum. We wanted him to be a part of a team environment so he could learn to socialize. Maybe I subconsciously felt it was my duty as a Dad to fix my son by placing him around other kids and I lost sight of the bonding aspect that comes with teaching the game. My Dad never had to worry about a developmental delay with me.

Don't get me wrong, I wanted to be the Dad that was super involved with my son. I saw everything play out in my head; it just did not manifest on a consistent basis. I can't understate the role of prayer and the true love of my wife to have the honest dialogue I needed. I had to realize God makes no mistakes. As my son gets older and we think about him being independent and transitioning into adulthood, I must take a hard look at myself. I missed a lot of opportunities, but, if I'm still breathing, there is still time to teach.

In recent months I have learned more about my Dad and who he was from my Mom, who was directly affected by his departure. Where I inherited her pain in the past, I have learned to forgive my Dad even more and thus allow myself to be a better parent. I applaud all the Black men who are refuting the stereotype and claiming their place as head of the household. It is vital that you are actively engaged with your children. Being present and not connecting with them does not make you a good father. To become a great dad, the traumas of a broken home must be addressed to not unwittingly become what you are trying to leave behind.

As Trey's parent, I am still his first teacher. This period of transition is critical. Not only is he changing physically, going through puberty, he will have to face new challenges and responsibilities that come with getting older. Our goal is to make sure we are doing enough for him to succeed, such as looking at sites that offer job placement for kids on the spectrum, preparing him to take the regents exam so he can work towards a high school diploma, even drafting a will to make sure we sustain him if something happens to us. We really valued the time we had with Trey at the height of the pandemic. We learned his strengths, his weaknesses, and it allowed us to work on what he needed to thrive.

We were blessed to finally get Trey into the right school where he was able to receive the individualized care and attention he needed. He is now receiving Applied Behavioral Analysis (ABA) therapy, something we could not afford when he was first diagnosed. He is learning the social cues necessary to survive on his own. At this time, we are waiting on approval from the Office for People with Developmental Disabilities (OPWDD) so he can learn vital skills including the sense of direction needed for him to travel on public transportation.

The goal is for Trey to be self-sufficient. He does his own laundry, makes his bed, washes dishes, and cooks his own food under adult supervision. He is thriving each day. When I think about where he started from, I can't help but be optimistic about his future.

My legacy will not be defined by how Trey follows in my footsteps. I will leave my mark by ensuring he is the best version of himself. Where he can exist as a boy who grew into a man who is a leader, capable of doing great things, and not characterized by a diagnosis or statistic.

Epliogue:
THE SPIRIT OF FEAR

Young Black men and women dying at the hands or gun of police is not a new phenomenon by any stretch of the imagination, but in the year 2020 it was never more visible. We heard about the deaths of Trayvon Martin, killed for having the audacity of walking to the store in a hooded sweatshirt for a pack of Skittles, Michael Brown in Ferguson, Missouri, Freddie Gray in Baltimore, Sandra Bland, but we never saw them executed live, with the exception of Eric Garner in Staten Island, who took his last breath while in the grip of an illegal chokehold, and Philando Castile in Minnesota who was recorded by his girlfriend moments after he had been shot by a police officer while sitting in his car.

While those public executions stunned us, we were so desensitized to the violence by that point that it didn't really cause a seismic shift in our consciousness. But 2020, already off to an abysmal start with the tragic death of NBA legend Kobe Bryant, his daughter Gianna and seven others in a helicopter accident, seemed to go completely off the rails. Not only were we exposed to a man-made virus that originated in China, leading to the first global pandemic in just over a century, the original American pandemic racism reared its ugly head yet again.

Emboldened by the inflammatory and divisive rhetoric of Donald Trump, racists were empowered to openly spew their hate. As evidenced, for example, in Charlottesville, Virginia in 2017 where a mob of white men marched with tiki torches ablaze, there was no more hiding behind white sheets and hoods with holes, these people did not care to hide their identity in this age of social media, advanced video technology, surveillance cameras on every street corner and building, and cell phone journalism.

In fact, it was cell phone video that brought to light the brazen murder of Ahmaud Arbery, the 25-year-old Black man who was attacked and shot to death by a white father and son while jogging through a neighborhood in Georgia. It was cell phone video that recorded the shooting death of Rayshard Brooks by a white police officer in the parking lot of a Wendy's after he offered to park his car and walk home after falling asleep in said vehicle. This suggestion was not good enough for the officer who escalated the confrontation that became physical when he threatened to arrest Brooks.

Arguably the most egregious lynching caught on video happened, also in Minnesota, on May 25, 2020, when George Floyd, a Black man, was handcuffed by four police officers and suffocated to death when one of the officers held his knee on Floyd's neck for eight minutes and 46 seconds. What made this so outrageous was that the officer in question knew he was being recorded and it did not matter to him. He did not even pretend to hide his contempt for the man who was begging for his life, screaming that he could not breathe, calling out for his deceased mother for help. Even as the final breath of life seeped out of Floyd, the officer kept the knee on his neck looking down at Floyd to make sure he was completely unconscious before lifting his body weight. It was something out of the National Geographic channel, except it wasn't a wild animal caught in the teeth of a lion or succumbing to the venom of a snake bite, this was a human being slowly dying with his face on the concrete.

This reprehensible act rightfully spurred a reckoning in our nation. I could only watch the complete video of George Floyd's lynching once. It was akin to the pictures I saw of Black men swinging from trees in front of a gallery of white men and children pointing and smiling like they were at the circus. It brought memories of the installation of the Emmett Till funeral at the Museum of African American History and Culture in Washington D.C. The 14-year-old Black boy killed by white men because he allegedly whistled at a white woman. A child. Walking through the installation immediately brought a lump to my throat. The uncanny likeness of the mutilated visage of Till lying in the open casket hit me harder than I expected.

I looked over at my boy, 10-years-old at the time, unaware of the poignant heaviness in the room he was standing in. Blissfully ignorant of the significance of this brutal act of hate. What really hit close to home was the mistreatment and ultimate death of 22-year-old Elijah McClain. Elijah was a young man living in the state of Colorado, who had a disability, and decided to take a walk to the store (sound familiar?). Someone called the police on him because he had a ski mask on.

What really hurt me to the core was the interaction between the cops and Elijah McClain. The first thing Elijah yelled out when he was being manhandled was that he was an "introvert". I don't know about you, but I am not aware of too many criminals that are going to yell out their social preference and proceed to talk about the things he does and does not put into his body when being apprehended. The heartbreaking part was that the cops were not even listening to Elijah's pleas. They were talking amongst themselves completely ignoring this young man beg for his life.

This total disregard for his life terrifies me with my own son. We can try our best to help him be more independent, yet once he walks outside, he is still a young Black man in Amerikkka. Add to that the inability to process information at the rate of speed necessary to perceive a threat, and it is a recipe for tragedy.

As a law enforcement officer, myself, I understand training in de-escalation techniques is taught as a recruit in the academy. But when your mind is already made up to inflict harm on a certain race of people regardless of the situation, there is no training that can reconcile racism and prejudice.

Trey came up to me on a Sunday evening and declared that "I'm a man now." His evidence: a 4x6 size copy of his 9th grade picture day photo, where he is smiling from ear to ear unashamed to display his brace-covered teeth, showing a full-grown mustache. He then directs my attention to the few curly black hairs sprouting from his chin.

"You and Mom think it is peach fuzz, but I'm growing a beard."

This made me laugh out loud. First off, Trey being able to communicate this was amazing, secondly, I recall when I was around his age being excited about some hair on my face. I was in college still trying to get my goatee to connect.

Being a parent is not easy. Being the parent of a young Black man is stressful. Aside from their health and safety, ensuring his physical, emotional, and mental well-being, in a world that is already judging him for being the wrong skin color, is paramount. I know one day I am going to have to let Trey venture out on his own. We are preparing him for what to expect when he has his own place to live. We want to ensure Aja will be able to live her own life without having the burden of taking care of her brother for the rest of her life.

For Trey to truly have some sense of normalcy, I must let him go. Now I have faith that he will survive because he can share his innermost thoughts. He can speak to me.

"For God hath not given us a spirit of fear; but of power, and of love, and of a sound mind." – *2 Timothy 1:7*

STATS

1 in 44 children are diagnosed with Autism.

Black children are FIVE (5) times more likely to be misdiagnosed or not diagnosed at all for autism spectrum disorder (ASD).

MY THOUGHTS

Symptoms of Autism are often unidentified in the Black community due to the lack of information and resources. Having a child diagnosed on the Autism spectrum is never the end of the world. These children are extremely brilliant and have a heightened ability to excel at certain things. Here are some suggestions on how to spot your child's special gift:

1. **Pay Attention to Heightened Senses** – while it should not need to be said that you should keep an eye on your child, it is vital that one with special needs is watched closely. For one, if he/she has difficulty communicating verbally, the other senses are automatically heightened and will be utilized to convey messages about his/her emotional state that are directly connected to the environment. Be engaged with your child. See what pictures, activities or sounds make him/her smile, laugh, or get excited. Verbalize to your child that you see how they are feeling and continue the dialogue.

2. **Be Aware of Signs** – Every child is different. Some may like to draw or dance. It may be a favorite subject, look for what they are interested in and expand on it.

3. **Keep An Open Mind** – Don't look at what your child is doing as an annoyance or hindrance. Show love and support for any evidence of a special talent.

Other books available from **Jamiyl Samuels**:

Pass The Torch: How A Young Black Father Challenges the Deadbeat Dad Stereotype

Children's books available from **The Amazingly Sensational Kids (T.A.S.K.)**:

The Amazingly Awesome Amani (Mascot Books)

The Amazingly Awesome Amani Takes On JITTERS & FEAR (Mascot Books)

The Sensationally Super Sandy (Mascot Books)

The Amazing Adventures of Awesome Amani – chapter book (T.A.S.K. Media)

The Amazingly Awesome Amani Battles the Molar Monsters (T.A.S.K. Media)

Where's My Daddy? (T.A.S.K. Media)

Are You Coming Home? – book 2 of Where's My Daddy? (T.A.S.K. Media)

I Miss My Daddy (He's in the Army) [T.A.S.K. Media]

Follow us online: https://www.TheAmazinglySensationalKids.com or https://www.wreachavoconline.com

Follow us on Instagram: **@TheAmazinglySensationalKids**
Follow us on Facebook: **The Amazingly Sensational Kids**
Follow us on Twitter: **@wreachavocwritr @T_A_S_K_Series**
Follow us on TikTok: **@TaskTikTok**

ABOUT THE AUTHOR

Jamiyl Samuels is an author, creative writer, screenwriter, and lyricist who always strives to make an impact with his work.

He began his college career as a Theater major at Morgan State University in 1996, but ultimately graduated with a Bachelor's degree in English and a Master's degree in Media Arts, with a concentration in screenwriting from Long Island University in Brooklyn, New York.

He is the co-founder of The Amazingly Sensational Kids (T.A.S.K.), a media company that utilizes children's literature to foster growth, promote literacy, creativity, and education through informed written and visual content & community engagement. He is also the founder of W.R.E.a.C. Havoc Enterprises – home to his adult literature, music, and film endeavors.

He was born in Brooklyn, but currently resides in Queens with his wife Tracy-Ann and two kids, Trey and Aja.

www.ingramcontent.com/pod-product-compliance
Ingram Content Group UK Ltd.
Pitfield, Milton Keynes, MK11 3LW, UK
UKHW020141300726
14059UKWH00008B/87